Value-Creating Growth

Thomas L. Doorley III
John M. Donovan

Value-Creating Growth

Growth

How to Lift Your Company
to the Next Level of Performance

Jossey-Bass Publishers
San Francisco

Jossey-Bass books and products are available through most bookstores. To contact Jossey-Bass directly, call (888) 378-2537, fax to (800) 605-2665, or visit our website at www.josseybass.com.
Substantial discounts on bulk quantities of Jossey-Bass books are available to corporations, professional associations, and other organizations. For details and discount information, contact the special sales department at Jossey-Bass.

Industry Print is a trademark of Deloitte Consulting. Growth System is a trademark of Deloitte Consulting/Braxton Associates.

 Manufactured in the United States of America on Lyons Falls Turin Book. This paper is acid-free and 100 percent totally chlorine-free.

Library of Congress Cataloging-in-Publication Data

Doorley, Thomas L.
Value-creating growth : how to lift your company to the next
level of performance / Thomas L. Doorley III, John M. Donovan. — 1st ed.
p. cm. — (The Jossey-Bass business & management series)
Includes bibliographical references and index.
ISBN 0-7879-4661-3 (acid-free paper)
1. Corporations—Growth. 2. Strategic planning. 3. Industrial
management. I. Donovan, John, 1960- II. Title. III. Series.
HD2746 .D66 1999
658.4'012—dc21   98-58116

FIRST EDITION
HB Printing 10 9 8 7 6 5 4 3 2 1

Contents

Part III: Reaching the Destination

To Chris, who gave a soaring voice to our work.

To our families, who give purpose to our lives:

Gail, you have always been special to me;
with you in my life, what a wonderful world!
Scott, your spirit has enfused this endeavor.
Rachelle, your creativity has enlivened
our prose. Dad, Lawrence Doorley, the only
one still standing and the first author,
your inspiration is here.

Judy, Shaina, and Rory, your love and
understanding inspire me, your relentless
support motivates me, and your charm and
mischief keep me happy. All are the right
ingredients to make things like this possible.

To not just one, but to the many givers
who bestow so much on us.
We are blessed by your support of us
and confidence in us.
You are why and how we grow.

The Authors

THOMAS L. DOORLEY III brings two-and-one-half decades of counseling to senior management on building tools and methods to drive sustainable growth. His clients span all major global economies. He founded Braxton Associates, then merged it into Deloitte Consulting, where it has continued to grow to twenty offices worldwide. He leads Deloitte Consulting/Braxton Associates' Global Growth Initiative. A frequent keynote speaker, he has led The Conference Board's programs on growth. He is coauthor (with Timothy Collins) of *Teaming Up for the '90s* and is a contributor to *The Wall Street Journal*, the *Harvard Business Review*, and *The Economist*. Further, he serves on the advisory boards of *The Alliance Analyst* and the World Economic Forum's Global Growth Companies Programme. He lives in Wellesley Hills, Massachusetts.

JOHN M. DONOVAN is Deloitte Consulting's global leader of Value-Based Management (VBM) and heads the firm's midwest U.S. strategy practice. As a leading practitioner in VBM, his clients span global economies. He is coauthor of the acclaimed book, *The Value Enterprise*.

Acknowledgments

Chris Doorley made this book a reality. A young, talented writer, he allowed us to continue to serve our clients and our firm. His task was to convert our hard-earned intellectual capital into a coherent, readable story. Thanks, CD.

The research and work with clients culminating in this book were made possible through the cooperative efforts of a team of people working shoulder to shoulder to unlock the secrets of value-creating growth. This team was constructed as a global group and has functioned effectively as such. Over the years, new members have joined the primary team and some have moved on. Because this was a team effort, we recognize its members.

We began our research in the spring of 1994. We chose growth as the topic after brainstorming a list of those issues of most importance to and least understood by our clients. Bill Ebeling, our valued partner, drove us to the focus on growth. We are grateful for his insight. Rick Smith, a partner at Deloitte Consulting, recognized the potential impact of the issue early and helped to galvanize support for the R&D side of our effort.

Throughout our work, we have been blessed with an unusually strong group of engagement managers. They are, in order of service, Jenny Topfer, Ken Carangelo, Mark Clark, and Josh Brand. Further, the analysts who have scrubbed the data and gleaned them for insight were especially capable. They are, in order of service, Geoffrey Willison, Matthew Marolda, and Brandon Prelogar.

In the early days, as we worked to build our intellectual foundation, Dan Ames, Rachel Burger, Jeff Macher, and John Marshall were instrumental. Throughout, John Penrose and Ed Gaskin, although never officially part of the development team, provided insight and were among the first to use and extend these new tools with clients. Mark Hernon, Barry Winer, and Amy Snyder were especially helpful applying the diagnostic to their clients.

The global perspective was enhanced by Jenny Topfer in Sydney, Simon Gifford in Johannesburg, Tony Themelis and Lucien-Charles Nicolet in Paris, Mark Lewis in London, Augustin Manchon in Toronto, and Naoko Hatakeyama in Tokyo.

In addition to the authors, the other ongoing source of energy, organization, and continuity was Janice Schneider.

A team works when it is a team in fact. The Growth Team works.

Our families and friends put up with weekends, nights, and vacations made less relaxing by our work and our initially underground manuscript. For, like many Valuable Formulas, this book was crafted on personal time for the first 90 percent or more.

Two others deserve special note: Janice, the outspoken, who all but challenged us to proceed, and Ken, who helped enormously, but he always gives a lot. And to all the others, such as Joan, who unanimously said, "Of course you can do it. Go for it!"

Cedric Crocker, our senior editor at Jossey-Bass, contributed a rare blend of insight, effective criticism, and enthusiasm. It kept us on track and confident.

Amos Tuck's Brian Quinn and Claremont's Peter Drucker provided important early benchmarks that convinced us we were onto something. Our firm provided funding for the research effort and, of course, support for taking this work to the marketplace.

Finally, although a solid research base was fundamental to give credibility to our learning, we also had to have extensive real-world testing. Our clients gave us this opportunity. As early adopters, they took some chances, but now relish their first-mover advantages. Thank you all for trying early and often. May you keep on building your growth systems and earning your just rewards.

Value-Creating Growth

Introduction

When seeking management advice, no client has ever said to a consultant, "If we hire you, could you help our company become mediocre?" Perhaps the next thirty years will contradict the experience of the past, but until then, we can assume that the leaders of companies in the future will strive for what they have always sought—excellence, high performance, and value.

In fact, if a company does aspire to a high level of achievement, it must grow. Companies with a near-fanatical focus on growth outperform all others—not marginally, but spectacularly. They achieve success by any measure. Consider these dramatic facts: (1) For shareholders, high-growth companies generate five to ten times the returns of slow-growth companies; (2) for customers, high-growth companies churn out new products and services at nearly twice the "normal" rate; (3) for employees, high-growth companies are the most satisfying places to work and, incredibly, job satisfaction soars despite enormous pressure to keep pace; and (4) for the economy, a small number of high-growth companies are the job-creating engines; in the last five years, a mere two hundred companies (less than 2 percent of all public companies) created 32 percent of all jobs.[1]

These four major stakeholder groups an organization serves can be used to distinguish a successful enterprise from an unsuccessful one. The organization must deliver: value to the investor who has shown confidence in it; value to the customer who purchases the product or service; value to the economy or community in which it exists; and value to the employees who fuel its productivity. To envision superior performance, we must view corporate achievement from this perspective and in these terms. These stakeholders' goals are universal, independent of the size of an organization and independent of its market. Delivering high performance in these arenas is the raison d'être for any business. This book will show you how to deliver on this promise through growth, which is the superior strategy for creating long-term value. This book provides a formula that can help you align all of the activities of your entire enterprise to support growth. We will embark together on the journey toward achieving value-creating growth.

To deepen our understanding of how high-growth companies produce such impressive results, four years ago we dedicated a team to research the drivers of success. Our team, sponsored by Deloitte Consulting, remains active today. We have been fortunate to draw on in-depth, firsthand analyses of some seventy-five companies— global companies of all sizes[2] representing all major industries from new technologies to manufacturing, telecommunications, publishing, and service sectors such as entertainment and finance.

Americas	Europe	Asia	
Ford	Ford	Nissan	Manufacturing
Cargill	Ecia		
Rodale Press	Rodale Press	Asahi Beer	Consumer
Sprint			
Midland-Walwyn	Cargill	National Australia	Financial
	Sofincor	Bank	Services
Hewlett-Packard			
Corning	Corning	Zenrin	Technology
Parexel	Parexel		

Exhibit I.1. Partial List of Companies Analyzed.

Some of these companies are listed in Exhibit I.1. As you can see, they cover the spectrum of business activity and regional economies.

In addition, we have drawn on secondary data from thousands of other companies and used the benefit of twenty years of successful strategic counsel to clients. In short, from all this experience and research we found that high-growth companies performed exceptionally well. We decided to write this book about sustained growth as a means to achieve these ideals, to provide the fuel that will sustain other organizations' journey toward growth. Thus, we offer you the first "takeaway" from our findings:

Takeaway

High-growth companies perform; they create value everywhere that matters.

Convincing as the case for growth is, it is not without trial. Our work has shown us the challenges as well as the benefits. Despite well-intentioned efforts, for the majority of companies growth remains an elusive goal that is hard to achieve and harder yet to sustain. For example, using a group of nearly two thousand companies over the twenty years from 1976 to 1996 as a case in point, the battle to maintain growth becomes stark. Of the companies in the top third in terms of growth rate from 1976 to 1981, fully 60 percent experienced ordinary growth (middle third) or low growth (bottom third) in the ensuing five years. By the final period, 1991 to 1996, only 15 percent of those who had started in the top third remained there. Thus, the odds of sustaining growth over two decades are about one in seven. Further, of the fast-growth companies from the first period that fell out of the top tier, only one in three managed to regain its high-growth status at any time in the period we studied.[3] Clearly, once a company topples from the high-growth zone, it will find it very difficult to regain its stride.

To compound the issue, large-scale growth is exceptionally hard to attain. When Jack Welch proclaimed his intention for General Electric to become the "first $70 billion growth company,"[4] he was not exaggerating by much. There is a growth wall at about 100,000 employees and/or roughly $50 billion in revenue that few have managed to climb.[5] Of course, this is problematic since, if growth is the focus, a company will evolve from a small to a medium to a large to an extra-large company over time. As the size of companies increases, we find fewer and fewer of them with high growth rates. These observations bring the bad news, and the one bad takeaway:

Takeaway

Growth is hard. It is a daunting challenge that must be attacked aggressively.

This fact should not be a surprise to any of us. In effect, the challenge presented by growth is analogous to that faced by teams or individuals who dedicate themselves to becoming World Cup champions, Olympic gold medalists, Pulitzer Prize winners, or Nobel laureates. Growing at a high rate does not mean being merely competitive, but thumping the competition. Being a fast-growth enterprise is by nature exclusive and elite, a status reserved for the few. Still, your company should not be deterred from pursuing growth any more than an NFL expansion team should be deterred from its Super Bowl aspirations. Growth has rules, a system, basic principles, and guidelines that we have identified in this book. Because there are basic principles, growth can be taught and growth can be learned. And again, the best news is captured in the next takeaway:

Takeaway

Growth is a learned competence. Any and all can improve at it.

To help you to develop a competence for growth, this book sys-tematically guides you through all stages of the journey. First, it lays the basic cornerstones for growth, then demonstrates how to diag-nose and overcome your own impediments to growth, and finally moves on to describe the end state—when growth becomes the process by which the company empowers itself, commanding its own evolution. We will unlock the secrets to value-creating growth by organizing according to a construct called the *Growth System*.

Within that system, basic components will help your organiza-tion react to challenges along the growth journey. These should be embedded deeply into your corporate identity and actions. Specif-ically, the Growth System is a set of processes and structures built equally on three solid cornerstones, shown in Exhibit I.2.

Cornerstone 1. The requirement for a deep *commitment* to growth. Value-creating growth does not occur by accident. A company must believe that growth is central to value creation and be dedicated to making it happen in order to succeed.

Cornerstone 2. Employing a *strategy* based on the *Valuable For-mula*. This innovative construct helps companies understand what makes their products and services special. It is designed to function across the phases of the growth cycle, the natural changes that dictate a company's growth and well-being. An understanding of how the Valuable Formula evolves can lead to long-term growth for a company.

Cornerstone 3. Developing the *capability* to sustain long-term growth. This capability is ensured by managing changes, con-tingencies, and potentialities. This cornerstone of the Growth System consists of an organization's ability to create, monitor, and nurture continually five growth-supporting foundations.

Exhibit I.2. Growth System Cornerstones.

These cornerstones comprise the Growth System, a paradigm that has enabled numerous companies to meet their growth goals. It is a working framework, not a classroom ideal or an untested model. Growth's promise to deliver value is proven every day, every quarter, every year, in the marketplace and in stock reports, in board rooms and brainstorming sessions. But success in growth has no end point or bottom line. It is not a mountaintop that caps the growth journey. Success is like a finely tuned engine that has reached maximum efficiency. Success comes when growth becomes the process by which a company conducts its business.

The unifying concept we term the Growth System has uniquely and consistently unlocked the secrets to value-creating growth for our client companies. Throughout, our unifying goal is to discover the keys to successful growth programs. Our consulting practice has focused on growth. The Growth System has been developed during this time, maturing into a comprehensive tool for attaining success across the four major categories: value to the shareholder, value to the customer, value to the employee, and value to the economy. No other approach to growth is holistic. Some stress growth strategies; others emphasize the importance of innovation or other key processes. Not one captures the systematic nature of what we have learned and now teach our clients.

The frameworks and tools we share in this book have been developed and honed in concert with our clients. These are the acid tests for a consultant: (1) Whether clients will use new ideas and (2) whether they work. They have and they do. We have worked with large-scale companies and new, small entrepreneurial enterprises, with publicly owned and privately held companies, and with clients from virtually all parts of the globe.

We have presented the Growth System to thousands of leaders like yourself—entrepreneurs, CEOs, managers—via hands-on work and through conferences. Our audiences have been receptive, inquisitive, and enthusiastic about the advantages of the Growth

System and by the prospect that these can be acquired through learning.

Response has been enthusiastic, particularly among Asian audiences, many of whom are struggling with growth for the first time in decades. In fact, their insight, which underscores the essence of the Growth System, is illustrated in this anecdote. Over dinner with colleagues in Tokyo, we described the results of a study conducted in Boston's Deaconess Hospital[6] that trumpeted what to the staff was a surprising result: Patients who prayed for recovery got better faster than patients who relied solely on medical treatment. To the three Asian business leaders at the table, this study gave no new insight. "There is no news there," they commented flatly. "Of course that is true. Everything must work together. We understand interconnectedness."

Consistent with such a holistic view, each of the three cornerstones of the Growth System—commitment, strategy, capability—carries equal weight and importance. It is a system in the truest sense. Balance and interconnectedness are the fuels of this engine, and no one part is greater than the whole. When asked, "Which of these components is the most important?" or "If you were to choose the one element I should focus on, which would it be?" the answer is straightforward: *Each element is critical.* Although you may initially construct your own Growth System by emphasizing some aspects over others, ultimately you must encompass all. Each is essential.

So begins our journey to deliver on our promise to our multiple stakeholders to achieve superior performance everywhere that matters.

Part I

Reaching the Destination

Aligning the Enterprise

Beginning the Journey

In the first stage of our journey, we will articulate and describe the basic characteristics your organization must have and practices it must follow to navigate the difficult path toward growth successfully. Certain foundations must be in place before your company can become one of the high-growth elite.

In Chapter One, we'll cover why it is important to grow for stakeholder value and the relationship between value and growth for shareholders, customers, strategic partners, and employees.

In Chapter Two, we'll discuss the differences between high-growth and low-growth companies and the three cornerstones for growth: commitment, strategy, and capability. *Commitment* is the will to grow throughout the organization; *strategy* is built on the Valuable Formula; and the *capability* to grow is established through five foundations: leadership, architecture, culture, processes, and knowledge.

Chapter Three covers commitment and ways to develop new products or applications, make acquisitions, expand geographically, and grow market share. Chapter Four explains the Valuable Formula in depth, from the core focus to a unique market proposition and the business system supporting it all.

Chapter Five provides a discussion of the foundations of growth in detail, with examples from our consulting practice and from common knowledge, showing the difference between high-growth and low-growth companies for each foundation. The attributes of each foundation are touched on.

1

Growth

The High-Performance Engine

Today, virtually everyone embraces the concept of growth. Numerous surveys (such as the Deloitte Consulting survey of Canadian CEOs or the Wirthin poll of their U.S.-based counterparts)[1] rank growth at the top of corporate strategic priorities. *The Economist*'s new survey of strategic priorities for the millennium[2] concludes that growth will remain number one three years from now.

In contrast, in the late 1980s and early 1990s, growth was not a strategic priority. Instead, a decided focus on getting more from less drove strategic initiatives. The American Management Association's 1995 *Change Management* report[3] represented the first citing of growth as an important corporate driving force.

How did this sea change happen? Company leaders began to recognize the obvious fact that shrinking, when carried to the extreme, results in oblivion. Experience demonstrated, painfully for many corporations, that one round of downsizing led to a second, and that round to a third, then a fourth. . . . After a decade of compiling convincing evidence against cutbacks and corporate anorexia, it has become apparent that businesses need to feed their engines; to expect more output (growth), more fuel must be injected into the engine.

Spectacular Performance Everywhere

Clearly, this renewed belief in growth is well-founded. The data overwhelmingly shows that companies that grow outperform their slower-growth counterparts dramatically, and do so everywhere that matters. High-growth companies create value—spectacularly so—across every dimension of performance and for all four critical groups of stakeholders: shareholders, employees, customers, and communities. Our analysis of the world's top growth performers for the World Economic Forum's 1998 Congress demonstrated how productive growth companies are.[4] The top seven hundred companies (out of a 30,000-company database) grew at 55 percent per year over a five-year span. The all-company average was a paltry 10 percent. The returns to investors of these companies exceeded the overall average by 200 percent. And, even within the already elite group, the top third created 50 percent more jobs than the bottom third. Clearly, these companies achieved impressive performance.

The link between growth and high shareholder value is not only strong, but universal. It is true for companies of all sizes and from all parts of the global community. Table 1.1,[5] showing data compiled from 1992 through 1997, demonstrates the change in annual market value versus revenue growth for companies in four size classifications, from those with annual revenue of less than $100 million to those with revenue in excess of $10 billion.

As the table shows, the smallest enterprises (revenue less than $100 million) with slow growth rates (under 5 percent) delivered negative returns to their shareholders. A sharp positive swing in shareholder value (10 percent) takes place at growth rates between 5 percent and 10 percent. As growth increased to between 10 percent and 15 percent, shareholder returns climbed to 15 percent. Finally, for those whose growth exceeded 15 percent, shareholder returns were 22 percent—more than double the 5 to 10 percent growth group! This comparison holds for each size classification. Fast-growing companies in the $100 million to $1 billion class realized more than six times the returns of their slower-growing coun-

Table 1.1. Payoff in Market Value for Growth.

		< $100 Million	$100 Million–$1 Billion	$1 Billion–$10 Billion	> $10 Billion
High	> 15%	23%	34%	34%	38%
Revenue Growth	10–15%	15%	19%	21%	23%
	5–10%	10%	14%	16%	17%
Low	< 5%	(1)%	5%	7%	15%

Company Size

N = 3,895 companies
Source: Compustat, Braxton Associates Analysis.

terparts; for the large companies ($1 to $10 billion), the rate was five to one; and for the companies with more than $10 billion in sales, growth at levels higher than 15 percent increased shareholder return by more than two-and-one-half times. Obviously, the payoff for growth exists for any size company.

It is important to note that the value-growth relationship is a well-defined natural tendency. Companies with high growth rates are most likely to have high returns to shareholders, and companies with low growth rates are likely to realize low returns. Figure 1.1[6] plots revenue growth and return to shareholders over twenty years for a group of one thousand companies headquartered in North America.

The relationship is strong between revenue growth and return to shareholders. The top right-hand cell contains the companies in the top fifth of growth and the top fifth for returns. (The size of the circles indicates the number of companies achieving the corresponding performance.) As with any economic condition, there are exceptions, but we have found that an overwhelming majority of companies conform to this pattern.

20-Year Profile—Companies Headquartered in North America

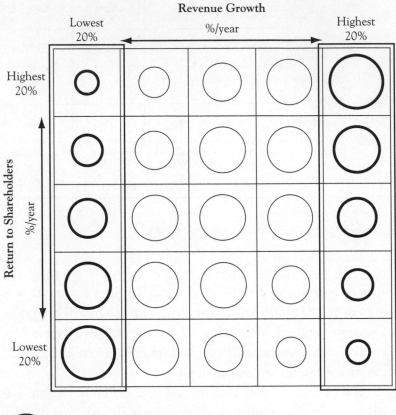

Figure 1.1. Relationship Between Growth and Value for United States
Companies.

Source: Braxton Associates Analysis.

To appreciate the power of the relationship between growth and
value, consider the two extremes, the low-growth companies in the
column on the left and the high-growth companies in the column
on the right. Obviously, it is possible to be a low-growth/high-return
performer; however, the odds are against it. There are six times as
many companies in the low-growth/low-return cell as in the low-

growth/high-return cell. For low-growth companies, low returns are the natural state. The inverse is true for high growth. There are nearly six times as many high-growth/high-return companies as high-growth companies suffering low returns. For high-growth companies, high returns are the natural state.

This tendency is not peculiar to American companies. The value-growth link is a global phenomenon. Figure 1.2[7] graphs value as a function of growth rate for companies in the Asian market. The pattern is the same as that in Figure 1.1 for North American companies. The European pattern would also look the same. All developed economies reflect the same pattern. Growth drives performance and value across the globe.

The concept that growth drives value is inherent, and we will refer to it frequently with the hope that the promise of value will be an incentive and an inspiration for you to pursue growth in your company. If creating value is your goal, then growth is the surest way to reach that end.

However, value to shareholders is not the only measure of success. Our findings also reflect increased value in terms of employee satisfaction. We followed one client's overall employee satisfaction rating from 1993 to 1996. As the company (a technology-oriented manufacturer of about $3 billion in revenue)[8] grew from 6 percent to 12 percent, the level of employee satisfaction rose from an indexed rating of less than 100 to more than 125, an increase of 25 percent. During the same period of time, we followed a second client, a $4 billion services company,[9] that had slipped well below its growth potential and was growing at just 2 percent per year in 1993. After committing to growth and implementing key initiatives to pursue and support it, this client grew from that lackluster 2 percent to a highly competitive 13 percent by 1996. Accordingly, their employee satisfaction index surged from 100 to close to 160, as shown in Figure 1.3. The 1997 results are just in, and growth is now 18 percent, with satisfaction in the 170 range.

The positive relationship between employee satisfaction and growth makes sense. Companies that are growing fast are beating

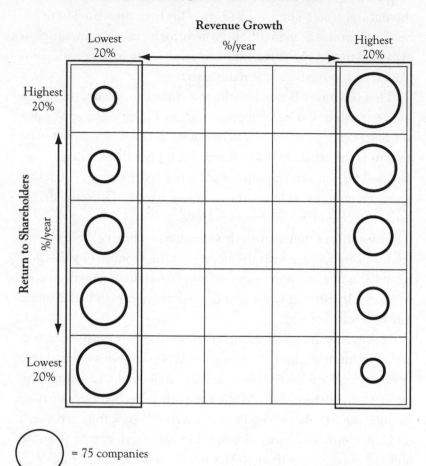

5-Year Profile—Companies Headquartered in Asia-Pacific

= 75 companies

Figure 1.2. Relationship Between Growth and Value for Asian Companies.
Source: Braxton Analysis.

out the competition and gaining market share. Employees share in this feeling of "winning." Also, opportunity abounds at fast-growing companies. Employees are challenged to improve their skills because the expanding business demands it. They are asked to take on more and different activities and are rewarded for doing so.

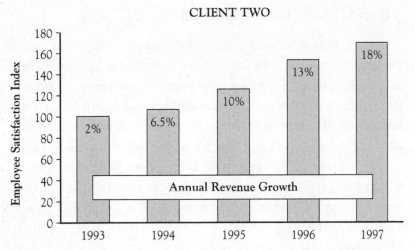

Figure 1.3. Employee Satisfaction Ratings as Growth Increases.

Finally, growth requires that the "cream of the crop" be hired and given the chance to perform. A fast-growing company cannot afford to hire anyone other than the best. These companies tend to respect performance and talent, independent of gender, race, or other characteristics not related to productivity. Their workplaces are remarkably diverse. All of these factors combine to increase employee satisfaction.

Another interesting phenomenon is the fact that employees complain about intense pressure—about having less time to do more and more. Yet they report high levels of satisfaction. This was a truly enlightening discovery for us—apparently, the harder we work, the better we feel.

All these factors comprise irrefutable evidence about the importance of a growth orientation. Our work over more than twenty years has made believers out of us. Sharing this information with clients has made believers of them as well. If the time has come for you and your company to embark on the growth journey, you too may be on the road to Nirvana. In your quest, remember that the growth engine drives performance and creates value for all stakeholders.

When Growth Is Not as Good

Without question, growth represents the superior long-term, value-creating strategy. But, in fairness, we have learned that growth is not the best strategic approach for every business at every stage of its evolution. Although a race car driver's end goal is to generate enough speed to outrun his competitors, it is not wise to accelerate constantly, particularly in a long race. The risk of accidents, blown tires, or overworked engine parts is too great. Wise strategies for winning incorporate pace into the equation. For example, as Donovan, Tully, and Wortman point out in *The Value Enterprise*,[10] growth can create value or destroy it, a fact that is shown graphically in Figure 1.4.

We will draw on the lessons we learned from researching this book to guide us on our own value journey. Our conclusions are similar to those of *The Value Enterprise*: Growth is the superior strategy for creating long-term shareholder value; however, not every business can generate value by growing all the time. We derive this somewhat contradictory statement from a simple observation: An investor only wants to increase his or her investment (that is, to grow it) if it generates an acceptable return. As a broad business principle, this level of return is the cost of capital. If a business is growing, but the returns are inadequate to cover the cost of capital, the investor must ante up again for a subpar return. Not likely. If a business is returning its cost of capital and more, the investor is anxious to add resources, thus compounding an attractive return.

Therefore, before committing to growing a specific business, determine whether or not its returns exceed the cost of capital. If you choose to grow a low performer in the hopes that it will power through the cost-of-capital barrier, recognize that it will destroy value as long as returns lag. When it breaks through the barrier, only then will it become a value creator. Also recognize the opposite side of this equation: Failing to grow a profitable business limits its value

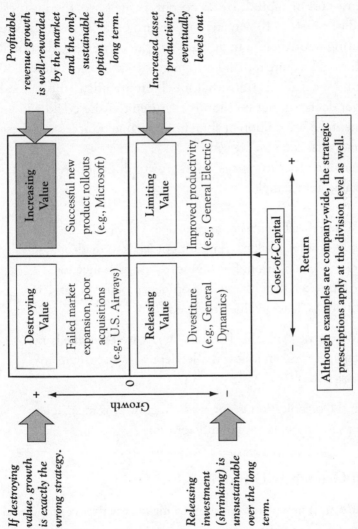

Figure 1.4. Examples of Growth Creating or Destroying Value.
Source: Braxton Analysis.

creation. A profitable business not growing fast enough in the exploit phase leaves value on the table, perhaps forever.

One of our clients once made this mistake. Returns were well above its cost of capital. By its corporate measure, the business needed to exceed a 20 percent cash return on gross assets. It was generating returns close to 50 percent. But achieving additional growth would require moving into markets with returns around 30 percent. "We can't sacrifice that much profitability," the general manager declared, but he soon recognized that he could add an incremental $500 million of shareholder value by accessing these other markets, doubling his growth.

There are other instances when growth does not create maximum value, for example:

- When the *commitment to grow* does not match the opportunity. Lack of commitment leads to inadequate resource allocation. Furthermore, low tolerance for risk, especially for large bets on new product or service offerings, leaves value untapped.

- When the "Valuable Formula" is not well-designed and competitors can follow the leader easily and trump any first mover.

- If the organization is not ready to grow or is incapable of sustaining its growth momentum.

When Growth Is Difficult

Of course, at times events conspire to make growth an exceptional challenge.[11] One such event is a cyclical economic downturn. Because we wanted to understand the growth-value link in both good times and bad, we purposely built our research base across long cycles, up to twenty years. In addition, our own careers span four distinct periods of economic downturn. From our experience with clients and from longitudinal analyses of company performance, we found that those companies that fought hardest to sustain their commitment to growth survived a recession in the best shape and thrived the most in the following return to prosperity. Although by no means inclusive, here are some of the initiatives that worked well for some companies during economic downturns:

- While conceding (but not without a battle) that *absolute*, actual growth could decline, they substituted *relative* growth measures to gauge progress. They targeted growth at greater than market rates and/or faster than key competitors. Thus, as growth slowed, they fought for and received more than their share of the market.

- They also took advantage of cheap capital when available to acquire low-cost assets, competencies, and companies.

- They identified their growth drivers and worked to protect them when under pressure to reduce spending. These fell into two broad categories:

  Key processes such as innovation and leadership development, and

  Long-term investments such as research and development (R&D), marketing, and employee development.

- They tended to slow down the rate of R&D investment but keep it in relationship to other measures, such as percent of revenue, recognizing that they would need robust growth processes when the economy turned around.

As these examples demonstrate, being cautious at times is prudent, but companies must never be stagnant. They must look forward optimistically to the future. While true at all times, this is most necessary in bad economic times.

Takeaway

Surround yourself with optimists:

- Avoid pessimists.

- Realists will find you.

Preliminary Conclusion

What can be concluded from what has been said so far is that growth is a complex management strategy with no simple truths save one: It is the best long-term strategy to create value. Obviously, short-term changes in businesses, markets, customers, economies, and so on will affect how a company executes its growth strategy. But contingencies for all these can be evaluated by and incorporated into a growth plan.

The chapters that follow explain the growth journey in three stages. The rest of Part I is a tutorial that lays down the three cornerstones on which the Growth System is built. Part II takes these principles and applies them to the real dilemmas facing companies that embark on the growth journey. We use a method called the "growth diagnostic." We will show you how to diagnose your degree of alignment with the model successful growth companies have used and how to pinpoint any impediments to your own growth. Part III deals with Nirvana—the end state in which growth becomes the process by which a company does business—and with how the future of growth will influence your company. We vividly paint a vision of a fully functioning growth company and explain how you can adapt that vision as your own.

2

The Growth System

Three Cornerstones of Success

How do companies achieve the spectacular high-performance promise of growth? How do they gain and sustain value-creating growth? We undertook a concerted effort to unlock the secrets of successful growth companies by doing the following:

- Creating a group of more than seventy-five benchmark partners worldwide to delve into their struggles and triumphs along the growth journey (a representative sample of companies in this group is shown in Exhibit I.1 in the Introduction)

- Building a global database of companies and their performance over five-year, ten-year, and twenty-year intervals. In this way, we were able to view the companies across economic cycles and as they underwent leadership, product, and strategic transitions

- Dedicating a research team to growth principles (in 1994)

- Working hand in hand with our own clients on growth issues for more than twenty years

Our research brought out sharp contrasts between high-growth and low-growth companies. Figure 2.1 summarizes some of these differences.[1]

As we synthesized our work and knowledge, we developed what we came to call the Growth System. We believe that this strategic framework is the key to sustaining value-creating growth. The system is comprised of three equally important, interlocking gears (cornerstones), as depicted in Figure 2.2. We found that, although a company can be out of balance for a time and rely on a compelling new product for its growth, as the company increases in size, all three elements—commitment, strategy, and capability—must be tightly aligned.

A simple way to view the Growth System is as gears in an engine. The Growth System's three basic gears (cornerstones) are commitment, strategy, and capability. We have also isolated the ten essential practices that comprise the three cornerstones. By fueling and maintaining these ten essential practices in your organization, you will make dramatic, continual progress for your critical stakeholders. The following paragraphs give some examples of the role each cornerstone plays in the Growth System.

Cornerstone 1: Commitment

What risk does a company take if it lacks full commitment to growth? Take as a hypothetical situation a company that has the capacity to grow at 30 percent per annum by creating a new, competitively strong product. But assume this company is overly cautious and unwilling to put its full efforts behind the pursuit of potential markets for the product. Rather than devoting extra resources to the product launch, it holds back. Because of this, the company may achieve only 10 percent annual growth. This lower figure may seem perfectly fine to management teams with less vision. However, not achieving as much as could be achieved is actually a failure. Hundreds of millions of dollars in revenue could be left untapped. Essentially, it's like driving a Porsche as though it were a Kia. The high-performance advantages of growth come from full *commitment*. Some actual examples of companies that have had a full commitment to growth are given in the following paragraphs.

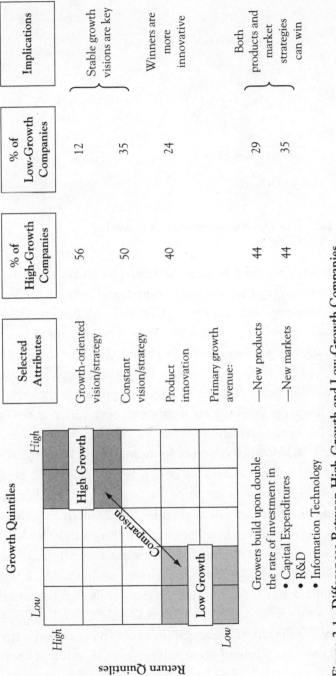

The following table presents the content from Figure 2.1:

Selected Attributes	% of High-Growth Companies	% of Low-Growth Companies	Implications
Growth-oriented vision/strategy	56	12	Stable growth visions are key
Constant vision/strategy	50	35	
Product innovation	40	24	Winners are more innovative
Primary growth avenue:			
—New products	44	29	Both products and market strategies can win
—New markets	44	35	

Growth Quintiles

High Growth

Low Growth

Comparison

High — Low (Growth Quintiles)

High — Low (Return Quintiles)

Return Quintiles

Growers build upon double the rate of investment in
• Capital Expenditures
• R&D
• Information Technology

Figure 2.1. Differences Between High-Growth and Low-Growth Companies.

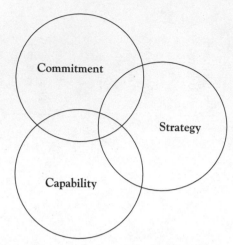

Figure 2.2. The Three Cornerstones of Growth.

Brunswick is a $4 billion recreational products company. Its brand names are well-known and powerful, and they are key leaders in the bowling and billiards markets. Brunswick's Boston Whaler is popular among power-boating enthusiasts; if one aspires to be a true ocean-going skipper, Brunswick's Sea Ray is the clear choice. However, in the early 1990s, the company languished, barely moving the growth needle. Brunswick CEO Pete Larson now has the company moving again. Perhaps his most significant contribution to the organization has been to reinstill Brunswick's will to grow. From his days at Kimberly-Clark and Johnson & Johnson, Larson knew the power of a growth strategy. Brunswick's 1997 revenues jumped 16 percent above 1996 revenues—a strong performance for a $4 billion company, and the first consistent double-digit growth in a decade. Brunswick is relearning the value of growth for its stakeholders.

At General Electric, the recognition that growth must play a more central role than it has in the recent past has led Jack Welch to go public with his commitment to growth. Welch has said that his goal is for GE to become "the world's only $70 billion growth company."[2] This public message reinforces the company's strong internal message. The end result will be that GE will find a way to grow. At GE and Brunswick, and at any company intending to grow over the long term, the commitment cornerstone must be firmly in place.

Cornerstone 2: Strategy

The second cornerstone is *strategy*. At the heart of any effective growth strategy is a robust Valuable Formula (discussed in depth in Chapter Four). The strategy must incorporate three elements: a sharp focus on the marketplace, a highly competitive proposition targeted at customer needs, and an efficient business system designed to satisfy customer needs efficiently. Without these elements solidly in place, products that are initially "hot" will wane as competitors trump them with their own new product offerings.

Some examples of the power of strategy include Apple Computer in the 1980s, especially its innovative Macintosh computers. The Mac set the pace early in the personal computer marketplace. For the first time, ordinary people, not just computer jocks, could learn to use this very user-friendly machine. In reaction to this innovation, the market exploded. Apple, a virtually unknown upstart, sailed upward, leaving IBM and many others in the doldrums. But Apple lost its momentum in the 1990s. The market the Mac engendered still fuels growth at 20 percent per year and higher rates than that for Dell, Compaq, Hewlett-Packard, and Gateway. Although Apple is recently showing signs of life, the organization is a mere shadow of its vigorous 1980s incarnation. Although there were many contributing factors to its loss of market share, the main reason was its inability to recognize what its Valuable Formula really was. At Apple, the goal was to build "insanely great machines." This goal, though catchy, did not tap the strategic essence of its Valuable Formula, which was that the Mac had the first-of-a-kind, user-friendly software operating platform. That was a Valuable Formula. The tremendous success and widespread dominance of Microsoft's Windows 3.1, 95, and 98 prove the worth of the original idea. Had

Apple repositioned itself to put its software into other people's machines, Microsoft might be facing a formidable opponent today. Instead, Apple misread its Valuable Formula, tied its software to its own machines, and allowed Microsoft the "window" of opportunity.

Today, Microsoft revenues exceed Apple's by 60 percent, and Microsoft sports a whopping twenty times Apple's maximum market value! Microsoft is a winner with $11 billion in revenue and a 33 percent five-year annual[3] growth rate because it claimed the software Valuable Formula for its own.

Sprint is an example of a company that recognized its Valuable Formula. Its SprintSense—a consumer long-distance offering—is a shining example of using the strategy cornerstone to fuel growth. Sprint has been able to outpace AT&T and MCI from the introduction of SprintSense in early 1996 until today. This is the value of a well-designed and well-executed strategic cornerstone.

Cornerstone 3: Capability

The third cornerstone is *capability*. Even with a strong commitment to growth and the good strategy of a Valuable Formula, the organization must have the capability to gain its full growth potential. Without the management processes and infrastructure to support growth, a fresh new product idea might capture only a fraction of its inherent potential. There are five foundations that must be in place to support an organization's capability for growth: leadership, architecture, culture, processes, and knowledge. These will be covered in more detail in Chapter Five.

Apple's history also serves as an example of the role of the five foundations in capability for growth. As noted, Apple's Macintosh revolutionized the computer industry. Despite its brilliant innovation, Apple did not do the pioneering work alone. Xerox built the Palo Alto Research Center (PARC), in northern California, with the express goal of researching new technologies in order to broaden its existing arsenal of copying and duplicating machines. The Palo

Alto Research Center came up with the basic idea that became the Mac. When set up in the 1970s, PARC seemed like the prototype of corporate innovation. Although the facility created new products, PARC was isolated. There were few, if any, growth-supporting foundations, for example, to link PARC to the company's headquarters in upstate New York. Ideas were hatched and nurtured, but PARC created revenues for other companies, such as Apple, because Xerox did not possess the *capability* to turn ideas into revenues.

Another example is Sequent, a rapidly growing supplier of sophisticated fault-tolerant computers, that in 1990–1991 came to an unusual decision for a young, fast-growing company. The company decided to reduce its rate of growth. Wisely, it recognized that it had only two of the three Growth System cornerstones in place. As an organization, Sequent was committed to growth and its strategy was based on a well-crafted Valuable Formula. The company was winning new systems competitions readily. However, it was beginning to miss the delivery dates promised to customers, and products were slower than projected to come on line. Rather than continuing down a hyper-growth path, Sequent backed off for six to nine months, focusing on building solid growth foundations for the future. Today, it remains a preeminent player in the marketplace.

An Expanded View

As the book unfolds, so too will the richness of the Growth System. In the diagram in Figure 2.2, the three cornerstones are very basic. Additional essential elements are introduced in Figure 2.3. The will to grow is fundamental to generating growth-sustaining companies. There must be a *commitment* to and a focus on growth.

The *strategy* cornerstone encompasses two new concepts. First, it is important for businesses to determine the essence of their winning product or service offering, which we call the Valuable Formula. Second, even the optimal Valuable Formula goes through a cycle. The product or service is created, taken to the market, and

Built on Three Cornerstones

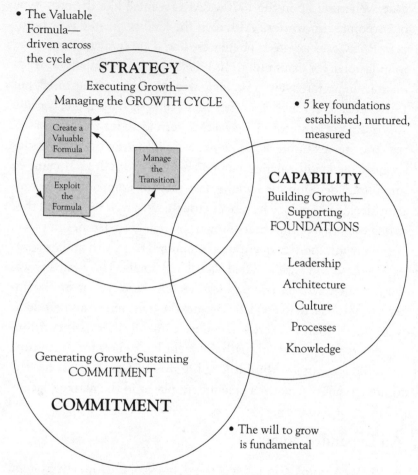

- The Valuable Formula—driven across the cycle

STRATEGY

Executing Growth—
Managing the GROWTH CYCLE

Create a Valuable Formula

Manage the Transition

Exploit the Formula

- 5 key foundations established, nurtured, measured

CAPABILITY

Building Growth—
Supporting
FOUNDATIONS

Leadership

Architecture

Culture

Processes

Knowledge

Generating Growth-Sustaining
COMMITMENT

COMMITMENT

- The will to grow is fundamental

Figure 2.3. An Expanded View of the Growth System.

exploited to achieve its maximum value. Then it must undergo a transition and be either refurbished or discarded for a new formula, which starts the cycle again with a new Valuable Formula.

Capability, the third cornerstone, is comprised of five growth-supporting foundations: leadership, architecture, culture, processes, and knowledge. These form the infrastructure that supports long-term growth. These components allow the company to reinvent itself, to sustain growth beyond a "hot" product or a charismatic CEO. Successful companies survive and thrive when their foundations are in place, monitored, and fortified as required.

Ten Essential Practices

Our goal in writing this book was to share our knowledge about growth in an action-oriented way—to teach you how to grow your company successfully. We have observed in our work that there are ten essential practices that are consistent across successful growth companies. Exhibit 2.1 shows these ten practices as they fit within the three cornerstones.

Chapters Three through Five deal specifically with each cornerstone and describe how to use the ten essential practices. So far, we have diagramed the growth engine. Our next task is to understand how the components work by watching them in action.

Cornerstone	Practice
Commitment	1. Believe deeply that growth drives value creation.
	2. Articulate a growth vision; embed it throughout the organization.
	3. Link growth performance to rewards and recognition.
Strategy	4. Create a Valuable Formula as a platform for long-term growth.
	5. Manage the Valuable Formula across the growth cycle.
	6. Globalize the Valuable Formula; maintain integrity and modify locally.
	7. Leverage two key strategic weapons— innovation and alliances—to exploit Valuable Formulas.
Capability	8. Identify and nurture all growth-supporting processes.
	9. Benchmark growth foundations vs. the "best of the best" and aim to beat them.
	10. Design and implement initiatives to align foundations.

Exhibit 2.1. Ten Essential Practices for Sustaining Value-Creating Growth.

3

Growth Commitment

The Will to Sustain Growth

When growth is done correctly, it is a long journey, a continuous challenge analogous to running a marathon—not chugging a diet drink, not buying an exercise gimmick, not following the latest fat-fad guru. Growth is for the long haul. *Commitment* is the effort that precedes the result, precedes the race itself, precedes the weekly regimen, precedes that first training step. Any marathoner must make a commitment to arduous training, scheduling, and nutritional preparation; he or she must risk injury and suffer self-doubt to complete the quest. Marathoners must want to go through it all because they believe in the journey and know that they will be stronger having undertaken the quest. The decision is identical for a company considering growth. You and your colleagues must truly believe that growth is important, that it is fundamental to achieving high performance and value, before you can tackle the inevitable obstacles.

Although the last decade of concentration on cost reduction and quality improvement yielded some impressive results, today's competitive challenge is growth and its intended result: creation of value. Growth has risen to be a primary strategic goal in the corporate mind-set, but unless you can commit yourself to the demands of growing, you will not be able to do what it takes to succeed. You must be willing to navigate through the pitfalls that ambush sustained growth. You must focus on the holistic nature of the system, which requires you to juggle the commitment, strategy, and capability cornerstones to manage a balanced whole. Commitment means sticking with R&D, marketing, or other high-investment programs. Commitment means hiring that stellar engineer while recruiting, even if you have already met your hiring budget and don't know exactly what you will do with her insight and energy. You must commit time and money to acquiring quality resources, because you will need them. Three practices crucial to commitment are discussed in the remainder of this chapter.

Practice 1: Believe Deeply That Growth Drives Value Creation

Our studies have shown that companies that grow aggressively are driven by their belief that growth is absolutely critical to their success. They have the marathoner's conviction that to achieve all the advantages they seek, in order to achieve value everywhere that matters, they must grow.

It would be ludicrous if the CEO of a high-performance company were to deliver a speech saying, "I am so pleased that we have had such rapid growth—some 25 percent over each of the last fifteen years. I never suspected that we could have done this, let alone over so long a period of time. I wonder how it happened. I am shocked at such an outcome!" Such serendipitous success is fantasy.

Growth is not an accident, nor a gift. Growth begins with a commitment to understanding and enacting basic principles and actions. To grow, you must mean to do so. You must have the will. You must be committed.

When we speak of "commitment," we are talking not about something the CEO and two or three vice presidents confer about. Commitment must be intrinsic and pervasive throughout the entire organization, echoed at every level by employees of all ranks and tenures. Commitment should extend from hiring practices to training, to promotions, transcending individual resignations, and continuing throughout the life span of an organization. Only such broad commitment endures. A company that plans to grow must plan to fuel growth through many decades, changes of leadership, and evolving markets.

Hewlett-Packard (HP), a high-performing growth company now in its seventh decade, epitomizes commitment to growth. Its CEO, Lew Platt, recognizes the bargain struck between HP and the high-talent people it seeks to recruit and retain. In essence, HP promises nearly boundless opportunity to advance based on the demands created by a growing organization. A growth company needs more people. Growth is so fundamental to HP that it builds the concept into its core statement of values, called "The HP Way." In recognition of how hard it is to sustain growth on a large scale (HP surpassed $45 billion in annual revenue in 1998), Platt commissioned a task force to study companies in which growth efforts have stalled to learn how his organization can stay on the path to continued growth. Clearly, commitment to growth is fundamental at HP.

What can you do if your leadership team and your company at large do not believe deeply in a growth strategy? First, you must build a convincing case for growth based on your company's special circumstances. Then share the concept broadly, thus winning buy-in and developing momentum for the idea.

Growth is such a common topic these days that building the case for it has become easier. In 1993, when one of our clients was struggling with barely GDP-level growth, it took a full year for them to commit to growth. The CEO appointed a senior-level team to address the issue. He called it the "growth task force." This task force engaged outside gurus, consultants, and facilitators. In the end, the team created a compelling story of how growth had driven value for others in their own and other industries and in their own history. The task force reported its findings at the annual senior management meeting, where the first stirring of commitment began. During the next year, concrete growth-supporting actions were initiated, for example, the company's innovation process was redesigned to streamline the development of new product ideas and the CEO crafted a new strategy with growth as the centerpiece. Today the company is committed to growing. Its value-creation performance is soaring, and its growth rate has surged into the high teens.

Pitching a growth platform should not take as long today. Still, you must ensure that your organization believes deeply in growth and has the will to grow. This is a precursor, an early step on the growth journey.

Practice 2: Articulate a Growth Vision; Embed It Throughout the Organization

One method to underscore a deep and lasting commitment to growth is to communicate it in writing. Call it what you like—a mission statement, vision statement, values statement. This manifestation of your intent can crystallize the concept and communicate it to others in the organization. Some may question the effectiveness of writing out such a statement, being skeptical from reading too many shallow, similar-sounding statements in both popular literature and corporate circles. But nearly 60 percent of the fast growers we observed have articulated a commitment to growth in writing. Only 15 percent of slow growers have done the same. So although forgoing a vision statement is not a terminal condition of all slow growers and mediocre performers, four times the number of fast-growing, high-performing companies have discovered the efficacy of drafting such a statement. Our recommendation to our clients is to follow the winning practices!

Two examples from our growth clients demonstrate such a commitment to growth with a clear vision of what defines their success. The first case is a $5 billion company that has increased its growth rate from 5 percent per year in 1992 to 20 percent per year in 1998. The CEO wrote the draft version of a vision statement in longhand, then passed it around his management team to gauge their reactions. His charge to his company is stated in terms of the growth culture he wishes to establish; it reads in part as follows: "To be acknowledged as the best in the world, we must continue to grow. We must grow by enhancing the quality and value of our services to our customers. . . . The culture and fabric of our company must include our expectation of growth. Our growth as individuals and a team will lead to growth in our revenues and create value for our shareholders." Many of the concepts implied by this particular statement are similar to Growth System concepts, such as the value proposition and establishing a growth culture within a company. (These will be featured in coming chapters.) We see here an intensely personal and aspiring commitment, which is central to any leader's statement. Furthermore, his comments follow the proper order of things. He makes the case for growth in the beginning and then outlines specific strategies to transform that commitment into action. He closes with a vision of the result.

The second example is a $3 billion division that has moved from barely growing at market rate three years ago to its current level at more than triple its competitors' average growth rate. The division CEO describes his organization's growth mission in these words: "To take advantage of our key assets, our brands, technologies, people, and alliances; to lead [key competitors] in profitable market share growth." Again, note the strong commitment to growth here and that it is supported verbally by a *strategy* for action. It is also specific. The question is, "How fast should we grow?" The answer is, "Faster than our competition; fast enough to gain market share." It would have been better for the CEO to have spoken of "value," to describe growth in market share, as growth promises value to shareholders, employees, economies, and customers. Nonetheless, the focus on outperforming the competition is clearly on target.

Your own pronouncements, however you wish to word them, should be made within the company and outside it. At speaking engagements, board meetings, or departmental meetings, through intranet, Web pages, broadcast communications, and memos, growth should be a recurring theme. Encourage your staff to verbalize it at every level. It is important to infuse the entire company with the organization's commitment to growth. This establishes the deep, enduring dedication to growth that lives beyond any transitory changes that may occur.

Practice 3: Link Growth Performance to Rewards and Recognition

This is where you will transform rhetoric into action. Promote growth by establishing measures and incentives to reward those who understand and pursue it successfully. This is called "walking the talk." Train new people for growth. Reward those who advance your company's growth with promotions, commendations, or "symbolic awards." These may sound shallow, but they work. For example, one day at 3M in St. Paul, Minnesota, I noticed very tacky gold plastic shoes posted on the wall in several offices. The symbolic award at 3M is called the Golden Step Award, modeled after the Greek messenger god Hermes' winged slippers. The award is given to people who take a new business idea and make it valuable, who initiate a new product or service and take it the necessary steps to create a profitable new market niche. As cheap and flimsy as the award seems at first, its value is intrinsic to the receiver, and the 3M staff believes in and covets it. You cannot be a true leader at 3M if you have not been part of a team that has won the Golden Step Award. 3M walks the talk.

Although such symbolic awards are effective, do not limit incentives to them. Other rewards could include anything from bonus programs (If it's important, pay for it!) to evaluations and promotions based on an employee's ability to enact growth, to social engagements at which growth is a subject of conversation. Find something that will work for you and your colleagues. The point is to find a method that takes your company's commitment and galvanizes the idea into an active strategy. Just be sure to measure and reward growth performance.

Keep Track of Progress Toward the Growth Goal

An important point, especially when you are seeking to reward employees, is to keep a running inventory of your progress toward your goal. Tracking your progress provides one more way to prove your commitment to growth. Self-evaluation and self-testing are appropriate. You can be your own judge. This book can provide a strategic framework for your efforts at sustained growth—a reference. But the industries, market trends, competition, or other variables specific to your organization will mean that you will face unique challenges that cannot be covered in this book. By experiencing these factors, you will become the best judge of your own success.

Create a Scorecard to Illustrate Your Progress

The Growth System relies on quick actions and reactions. Because competition defines growth, beating the competition requires the alertness and efficiency that come from autonomy. You must decide what concepts and constructs allow you to streamline your reaction to market changes. Commitment to growth is essential. So, gauge the strength of your commitment by examining how your organization measures up. Create a scorecard like the one in Exhibit 3.1 to show your status and progress.

An affirmative answer in every category would be a superlative scorecard, to be sure, but certainly not essential. The trick is "just do it." Analyze where you can improve in each category, and then work on it. For instance, perhaps your management team always discusses growth, but the discussion takes place at the end of long meetings. That's not as good as if growth is discussed early on the agenda and is a prominent theme that guides team discussion.

Commitment may be simultaneously the easiest of our three cornerstones to conceptualize and the most difficult to execute. Bob Edmonston, group vice president at Morton International, has described his company's commitment to growth. Most of Morton's core markets are mature and face low projected basic material

---

Practice 1:
Believe Deeply That Growth Drives Value Creation

- Is the growth message understood and acted on at all levels, within all divisions and functions?

- Is growth an important agenda item at all management team meetings?

- Can you list specific actions being taken to drive growth?

Practice 2:
Articulate a Growth Vision;
Embed It Throughout the Organization

- Does a well-accepted statement exist underscoring the importance of growth?

- Do internal and external communications highlight growth efforts and results?

Practice 3:
Link Growth Performance to Rewards and Recognition

- Do formal measurement and reward systems explicitly incorporate growth? Are these systems understood?

- Are any symbolic awards tied to growth efforts and results?

Exhibit 3.1. Commitment-to-Growth Scorecard.

growth rates. For example, one of Morton's producing salt mines in Spain was developed initially by the Romans. Its cash flow in the fifteenth century financed Columbus' trip to the New World—an incredibly mature business! Edmonston's own specialty chemical

- Develop new applications for existing products, technologies, and processes.

- Expand geographically as soon as a new Valuable Formula proves itself.

- Grow market share everywhere, all the time.

- Execute tactical acquisitions to leverage existing competitive positions.

- Continually introduce new products well in advance of competitors or even customer request.

Exhibit 3.2. Five Growth Initiatives at Morton.
Source: Bob Edmonston; The Conference Board.

divisions face a modest growth rate of 2 percent, yet the company grows at nearly 10 percent per annum. How can that be so? We believe this is because Edmonston has articulated five growth-based strategic initiatives that he and his team rely on to trigger growth above market and competitor rates, as shown in Exhibit 3.2.[1]

In addition, Edmonston notes wryly that "at Morton, there is an expectation of growth. If you can't find a way to grow your business, the company will replace you, the business, or both." In the hyper-growth world of high tech, we have seen that Hewlett-Packard is committed to growth. In the modest-growth world it operates in, Morton is equally committed to growth. These two companies represent benchmarks as you assess your own company. Are you as committed as they? If so, you are ready. Let's move on to discovering your own Valuable Formula and learning how to build and manage it.

4

Growth Strategy

How to Build and Manage Your Valuable Formula

Every executive with more than a few years of leadership experience has had this nightmare: You are standing in a vacant office long after work hours. Examining a depressing cash-flow statement, you are plagued by your company's shortcomings. But you are confused about what could have averted the disaster and even more at a loss as to how you can resurrect your failed strategy. Staring at figures reflecting much of a year spent in the red, you can identify when it happened, even which competitors eclipsed you. But one question is left on your lips: "How did we lose our edge?"

Two words summarize how you fell behind and how you will get ahead: *Valuable Formula.* Whatever business you may be in—telecommunications, financial services, oil and gas, chemicals, consumer products—this phrase belongs in your lexicon. For any product or service that your organization offers to its customers, the *Valuable Formula is the key strategic concept for gaining and sustaining a high-performance advantage.* It is the fuel that drives your growth engine. The Valuable Formula is already at work for you, whether you have identified it as such or not. The challenge that you face when using the Growth System is to design and manage your formula effectively. Successful growth companies that we have encountered develop their Valuable Formulas to launch and then propel their success. Every company has these formulas; they build them, globalize them, and change them. Dell Computer's annual revenue growth thus far in the 1990s exceeds 50 percent. It reinvented the computer industry via its Valuable Formula based on direct sales. Intel, at more than $20 billion in revenue, continues to grow at 30 percent per year (over the past five years) by a technology-driven Valuable Formula that continually presents its customers with simultaneously more powerful, faster, and cheaper computing power. And Starbucks is aggressively rolling its coffeehouse Valuable Formula across the Americas, growing at 60 percent per year, while their old-line competitor, Chock-Full-O-Nuts, struggles to grow at all.

Practice 4: Create a Valuable Formula as a Platform for Long-Term Growth

Successful growth companies realize that a truly Valuable Formula adheres to two rules: (1) A well-crafted formula is a clean representation of *focus*, its *market proposition*, and its *business system*, and (2) the formula must be managed across the three-phase *growth cycle*. To clarify both requirements of the growth strategy, let's begin with the concept of the Valuable Formula itself, which is the antidote to that nightmare.

Our clients have come to celebrate and employ the Valuable Formula strategy for their product and service innovations and to advance their own growth. First think of the Valuable Formula as a constellation, as shown in Figure 4.1. At the hub is a core statement of focus, with ten core elements connected to it by spokes. Each core element is one of the tools you can use to bring your formula to the marketplace.

The dotted line in the figure represents the dividing line between the *market proposition* (what the customer sees and is influenced by) and the *business system* (those components of which the customer is largely unaware). Although the business system may not be visible outside the organization, its existence is as essential to growth as the market proposition that the customer can see. An analogy is a cruise ship. Above the water line are the cabins, the

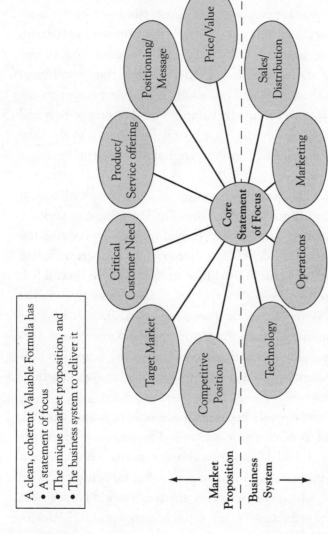

A clean, coherent Valuable Formula has

- A statement of focus
- The unique market proposition, and
- The business system to deliver it

Market Proposition

Business System

Positioning/ Message

Price/Value

Product/ Service offering

Core Statement of Focus

Sales/ Distribution

Critical Customer Need

Marketing

Target Market

Operations

Competitive Position

Technology

Figure 4.1. The Valuable Formula Model.

deck, and recreational amenities such as the pool, bar, and ballroom. These are the ship's visible market proposition. Below the water level are the ship's business systems: crew quarters, engine room, bilge pumps, propellers, and ballast tanks. Although most passengers are unlikely to spend much time considering what goes on below deck, the market proposition is clearly sustained by the quality of the "below deck" business system. If the ship were to have an outdated engine, a rusted, leaky hull, an inadequate crew, or any other "invisible" deficiencies, it would detract from the overall Valuable Formula—the leisure and peacefulness of an expensive cruise. In the same way, only an equally balanced market proposition and business system will ensure that your boat will stay afloat in the marketplace. An imbalance will result in an inability to create revenue, growth, and value.

Boston Beer Company is an example of a company with a clear focus at the heart of its Valuable Formula. The company seeks to satisfy discriminating beer drinkers (target market) by brewing the best beer in the world (focus). Another example, America Online (AOL) offers low cost, unlimited Internet access with special features and a user-friendly system, thus creating a distinctive market proposition. SAP represents the prototype of an effective business system incorporating its own software design and development, buttressed by strong alliances with systems consulting firms that provide customized enterprise-wide information technology solutions and implementation.

America Online nearly became an example of failure through misalignment of its market proposition and business system. At the end of 1996, AOL had developed a very competitive and contemporary market proposition. It introduced a flat monthly rate with suitable fanfare, which created a very enticing market proposition, anchored by the attraction of unlimited Internet access. Unfortunately, their offer was not supported by an equally well-developed business system. Ironically, so many people bought into their market proposition that members found their "unlimited" access routinely blocked by an overload to AOL's operating system. This revealed a defect in their "invisible" mechanisms as thousands upon thousands of new and established users found it impossible to get online during normal waking hours. By not being able to deliver on its promise, AOL's formula lost much of its value. In response to customer complaints, AOL shored up its underpowered business system and pledged to invest $500 million or more on top of their existing network capacity. Later on, of course, its CompuServe/ WorldCom alliance helped to resolve the problem. Although the company has maintained its position as the leading consumer Internet service provider, the lesson is: Ensure that you have the requisite business system to deliver on your distinctive market proposition. Don't make the same mistake that AOL did.

In contrast to AOL, pharmaceutical firms have highly efficient business systems, which allows them to shuttle new drugs through the complicated FDA approval process and to educate doctors and consumers about the benefits of upcoming over-the-counter and prescription options. However, as their traditional technologies age, they have found themselves lacking in new product development compared with biotechnology firms. They have sometimes struggled to create new market propositions (new drugs) to take to their consumers. To balance their Valuable Formulas, some pharmaceutical manufacturers have allied with biotechnology firms, such as the alliance between Hoffman-LaRoche and Genentech. By employing biotechnology companies' skillful product innovators, the pharmaceutical companies are joining their effective business systems with the biotechnologists' proven capacity for crafting market propositions.

As important as it is for your customers to believe in the formula, you and your colleagues must "buy into" or believe in it as well. Like a company's concept of growth, the Valuable Formula must make sense in context, not just be something being sold. The Valuable Formula provides the basis for the growth management framework—the "growth cycle." A company's Valuable Formula should be a clear representation of three things: *focus*—a simple, tangible market niche, innovation, or customer need that establishes a unique goal the company can offer and excel at; the *market proposition*—what the customer sees; and the *business system*—what the company provides. All elements must be in balance. For example, a low-price product offering must build on a low-cost structure and highly efficient distribution system. A complex product offering must be able to draw on an extensive post-sale service network. Some specific examples of these principles in real life follow.

Example 1: "Brewing the Best Beer in the World"

Let's return to the Boston Beer Company. The company's Valuable Formula is the distinctive taste and consistent high quality of the beer it supplies, a beer whose inception coincided with, or perhaps triggered, an explosion of the micro-brewing industry. Renowned and acclaimed internationally, Samuel Adams' market niche is so pervasive that you see the face of the "brewer/patriot" who inspired its name smiling from atop tap handles in your local brew house, and everyone else's.

This wide-reaching success would not have been possible without a clear focus. As noted earlier, founder Jim Koch intended to brew the "best beer in the world." When he began his quest in the mid-1980s, it must have seemed outrageous, as do most Valuable Formulas—they are ambitious, far-reaching, and often seem incredible at the outset. Prior to his decision to launch Sam Adams, Koch had been a consultant. Thankfully, he chose to become the world's best brewer instead of the world's best consultant. If you were to ask him why he changed professions, he'd tell you something akin to, "Perhaps it's in my genes, but I'm a brewmeister. My father and uncles were before me, and theirs before them."[1] However, being able to brew the best beer in the world is not a function of genetics. Koch took calculated steps to create his Valuable Formula.

His focus was on a great tasting beer. This compelling focus involved myriad provisions: crafting a masterful recipe, perfecting the brewing process, acquiring the best available ingredients, and on and on until he achieved a taste he was satisfied with and that he was confident would sell well to patrons. All of his preparations come together to create the first part of his Valuable Formula: a great tasting beer. His beer dominated those beer-tasting contests in Colorado and elsewhere.

Next Koch had to exploit his formula, to take it to consumers. He employed as many people as he could to do this. He hired a very large sales and marketing staff to visit bartenders and other beer purveyors individually, suggest they stock Samuel Adams, and convince them that the superior quality of the product warranted the price being a dollar or two higher than that of a mass-produced domestic lager. Because Sam Adams had been judged to be the best, this contributed greatly to its reputation and broadened the consumer base. Thus, building out from his focus, Koch fleshed out the core elements in his Valuable Formula. Because he crafted the best recipe, it required the highest quality ingredients. Because the ingredients were expensive, a high price was required. Because the beer was made of the best recipe and ingredients, it won awards. These accolades helped justify its high price to new consumers, thus reducing post-purchase dissonance, and so on.

How successful is Koch's Valuable Formula? One striking measure of his success is that the Boston Beer Company enjoys about six times the market share of its nearest micro-brew or craft-brewed competitor. Another is its five-year growth of 60 percent per annum. People seem more than willing to imbibe Samuel Adams' despite the sharp markup over other domestic brands. Competitor response is typified in the ad campaigns by Miller Brewing Company, which declare plaintively, "It's Time for a Macro-Brew!" Clearly, Koch has found his Valuable Formula, a formula with a clear focus.

However, the Valuable Formula at the heart of Samuel Adams is certain to come to an end, as they all do. At that point, Jim Koch will have to evaluate where the value of his formula is being compromised. Maybe there will be price resistance, so perhaps the adjustment for Boston Beer will be along the price/value spoke shown in Figure 4.1. Maybe micro-brews will prove to be a fad. Whatever the case, Koch will either fine-tune his present Valuable Formula or transition into a new Valuable Formula. We'll see later how this might work.

Example 2: "Creating the Ultimate Movie Experience"

Next, let's envision a Valuable Formula that has not been implemented yet. Unlike Koch's formula, this one is very early in its development, just beginning to test the market. The idea is to create the ultimate moviegoing experience, which is also a bit less tangible than a great-tasting beer. What does "the ultimate movie experience" mean? Though focused, the concept is a bit esoteric. A theater chain might try to create a moviegoing environment that customers prefer to any other. Instead of sitting down with the newspaper and saying, "I want to see a movie. Where is *Citizen Kane* playing?" Ultimate Cinemas wants you to say, "I want to see a movie. Let's go to Ultimate Cinemas and see what's playing." Again, we see that the Valuable Formula is an ambitious, arguably outrageous goal.

Can this goal be accomplished? We don't know yet. That remains for Ultimate Cinemas to discover, again via the marketplace. But we do know from working with Ultimate Cinemas' team that they have a clear focus and a prospective market proposition. They have identified a customer need and their target market, and they now have to put the rest of the elements in place. They know what active moviegoers want and now need to refine their message so that customers in this target market know Ultimate Cinemas delivers what they want. The business system must be honed so that every theater employee upholds the standard—creating that ultimate movie experience. The company knows it wants to provide the best cinematic setting, just like Jim Koch wanted to brew the best beer. But, what's in Ultimate Cinemas' recipe? Ultimate Cinemas' theaters feature the best sound systems and technology, have comfortable seating, offer food and beverages beyond popcorn and soda, provide efficient and courteous service, and are housed in a safe, clean, easily accessible home away from home. There is a focus, and the Valuable Formula is being crafted. What remains is to test it, fine-tune it, then exploit it—a concept reserved for the next section of this chapter. Good luck to Ultimate Cinemas. Let's watch to see how it goes and, as moviegoers, hope for success.

Example 3: "Revolutionizing Telecommunications Technology"

You may remember the slogan at the heart of Sprint's first market proposition: "So clear, you can hear a pin drop." In the early 1980s Sprint was the first company to convert to an all-fiberoptic network, which delivered much higher quality voice transmissions. Copper cable, the competing technology, was frequently scratchy and unclear. By leaping ahead of the competition, Sprint focused its Valuable Formula on a high-quality promise to its customers. The company had gotten to the technology first, and customers bought its product. Because of the simply communicated "pin-drop" image, built upon a business system of superior technology, Sprint grew. This Valuable Formula—distinctive in the eyes of the customer (market proposition) and superior to the competition (business system)—was a winner.

These three cases illustrate that the Valuable Formula is the strategic essence of growth.

Takeaway

The Valuable Formula is the strategic essence of growth. It is the platform for long-term strategic success.

The Valuable Formula is simple, direct, and easily articulated. Can you articulate your company's Valuable Formula? Can you express it briefly in terms of the model as shown in Figure 4.1? If you cannot explain your formula with the diagram as a guide, nor state your focus succinctly, your formula may need some work. It is crucial to make it simple so that it passes what we call "the elevator test." A Valuable Formula that cannot be expressed between two floors on an elevator ride needs more focus. If you have a broad concept with little focus, the initial spirit and intent of your Valuable Formula may become confused or lost as it goes through fine-tuning and the exploit phase. In addition, your market proposition and business system may be jumbled and incoherent, making it difficult to manage challenges in the marketplace. A well-articulated Valuable Formula allows you to identify specific threats to your product in the marketplace. Focus your vision clearly and early, and use it as a beacon later.

Simply writing one's formula is not enough. That would be the triumph of form over substance. Whether a formula is valuable depends on whether or not it is a winning, coherent package. If you can describe it plainly, you are more likely to understand what drives its success and thus improve your ability to know when to make needed changes. In essence, you gain control.

Practice 5: Manage the Valuable Formula Across the Growth Cycle

When based on a focused Valuable Formula, the growth cycle is a succinct three-part process. Envision a cycle with three phases: first, *creating* the Valuable Formula; second, *exploiting* the formula; and third, *transitioning* between old and new formulas. These phases begin again when a company discerns that its formula has lost its value. Ironically, though the cycle is born with the creation of the Valuable Formula, the challenge in mastering the three phases is to have the courage to destroy that formula. When a strategy has limited value, you must either change it or move to the next creation phase and embrace a new one. Of course, some companies cling to a Valuable Formula and ride it into the ground. We don't recommend that strategy to any of our clients. In addition to managing their Valuable Formulas effectively, companies that are able to sustain growth understand that all Valuable Formulas flow through a cycle and are prepared to manage all three phases of that cycle.

Takeaway

All Valuable Formulas flow through a cycle. Be prepared to manage all three phases of that cycle.

As we've said, the Valuable Formula represents the best product or service offering you can present to your customers. However, although you may have great success in inventing a Valuable Formula and in exploiting that formula to gain prominence in the industry, its value is transitory. Even the most ingeniously crafted, effectively executed Valuable Formula is mortal. Every business will eventually have to manage the *transition* from one formula to the next. Competition, changing customer needs, and evolving industries dictate that there will be a limited life span to each product or service your company can offer. Realize that the eventual death of your formula will come—by unforeseen technological advances, government intervention, or the efforts of those pesky competitors. It will happen! Whatever the cause, your own experience has taught you to know that your product is destined to be consumed by the market. The key to commanding the Growth System is to manage the three phases of the growth cycle, as depicted in Figure 4.2.[2] Instead of waiting for competitors to devour your product, cannibalize it yourself and preempt a loss in market share, revenue, and customer/brand loyalty. Remember that *the key to the Valuable Formula is understanding when it has value and when it does not.* Be proactive about re-creating it, and you won't have to react to its destruction by competition.

We have overlaid the names of some companies that represent each of the phases of the growth cycle in Figure 4.2. Within the "create" phase (represented by Corning), a company's innovators will be the ones to divine a focus. This focus is at the center of the

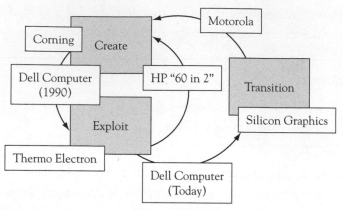

Figure 4.2. The Growth Cycle, with Representative Companies at Each Phase.

Valuable Formula model. If the creation was done by a limited number of executives, technical, and creative people, then the following phase, exploiting the formula, must involve virtually the entire company. Everyone must work together in the "exploit" phase (as shown by Dell Computer at the beginning of the 1990s and Thermo Electron) because this is the period during which your company will achieve its peak value creation, peak revenue growth, peak earnings, and peak job creation. Everybody must work together to take advantage of the company's unique promise, take your product and/or service to the customer, and achieve dominance over the competition. One of our clients has described this phase crisply. For over a decade he has been the final speaker at all of his company's new-employee training seminars. He closes by saying, "Hopefully, you've learned much about us and will carry that knowledge with you. As you leave here to serve our customers, I want you to remember one last thing: 'Execute, don't add!'" In the exploit phase, he is exactly right.

Now let's discuss the nuances of the growth cycle. As Figure 4.2 shows, there is a large cycle from creation through exploitation to transition with a tighter circle inside that. This smaller circle represents fine-tuning of the Valuable Formula. When you take your

Valuable Formula into the marketplace, some deficiency may come to light: a price/value error, a miscalculation in target market, or a sales/distribution limitation. For instance, if going global, you may have to adjust for special local market conditions. In exploiting the formula, you are simultaneously testing it against actual customer response or sales and distribution efforts. You may need to operate in the tighter tuning circle for awhile, testing and honing your Valuable Formula before real profit and value can be attained. Hewlett-Packard's growth challenge of generating 60 percent of its revenues from products introduced in the prior two years ("60 in 2") serves to drive this part of that cycle. By aligning either the elements of your market proposition or your business system during this phase, you will be better able to exploit your Valuable Formula. You must achieve a balance between "visible" (market proposition) and "invisible" (business system) elements.

You may need to refine the formula a number of times, as we saw earlier from the examples of America Online and the pharmaceutical companies. Recall that, although focused, those companies' Valuable Formulas were not balanced, so they could not excel. It was necessary for them to analyze the core elements that made up their products and services. After identifying the flaws, the organizations put significant resources and effort into rectifying their deficiencies—in effect recreating their formulas and realizing their full value.

After having moved successfully within this fine-tuning circle, you must drive single-mindedly toward exploiting the Valuable Formula. This is the phase in which your company achieves its peak revenue, market share, and job creation, and not surprisingly endures the greatest demands on your time and effort. To return again to the cruise ship analogy, the exploit stage is when you must put your company's engines on full speed ahead. Always inextricably linked to the exploit phase is managing the transition when the formula loses value. The large arc connecting these two stages (Dell Computer today) is bridged by anticipation and preparation as changes occur. Then you must power through the transition and move back to the creation stage (as shown by Motorola's transition from analog to digital technology).

Now let's return to the Sprint case study. Having successfully exploited the advantages of their technological supremacy for nearly a decade, by the early 1990s Sprint found itself being swallowed by competitors. The uniqueness had gone from the all-fiberoptic network as key competitors matched the technology. The exploit phase had ended, and Sprint needed to manage a transition to a new Valuable Formula.

Example of Managing the Transition: "Simplifying Long-Distance Savings"

Sprint was losing the long-distance market it had previously won. The primary foe, industry juggernaut AT&T, after about a decade of quiet stagnation in the long-distance market, made a concerted commitment to recapture industry supremacy. Their efforts were a success. Sprint also had strong competition from the effective marketing tactics of MCI, a competency MCI had been leveraging since that company's inception. Sprint Long Distance President, Gary Forsee,[3] after analyzing his division's recent performance, expressed the situation this way: "While we occasionally enjoyed a sharp jump in growth, we weren't sustaining it. Our theme of high-quality voice reception no longer was working for us."

The answer Forsee sought would become the focus for Sprint's new Valuable Formula. Sprint decided that the biggest problem facing long-distance service was the complicated pricing plans that characterized the industry. Although companies could readily quantify daily and hourly rates, the consumers could rarely understand them. Remember how many times a new long-distance carrier called with new long-distance offers?[4] They usually called during the Final Jeopardy question, which was as irritating as their complex fee plans. They would say something like, "Mr. Doorley, this is

Sue Ellen with Dakota Telecom, and we'd like to offer you our new Penny-Saved package."

In a rush to catch the Jeopardy clue, and already a customer, I'd say, "That sounds great, Suzie. Sign me up."

A few months later I'd receive another call, this time during dinner. "Mr. Doorley," came the solicitous voice, "this is Scott with Dakota Telecom, and we'd like to offer you our new Penny-Earned package."

"Penny-Earned? I thought I was on Penny-Saved. What's the lowest pricing plan?"

"Well, as opposed to Penny-Saved, which I'm sure you're familiar with, your rates with Penny-Earned are 6 cents per minute on Saturday mornings, 22 cents per minute on Sunday afternoons, 12 cents a minute on Monday nights after five."

I didn't want to waste time figuring it out. My dinner was getting cold. "Tell you what, Scott, my friend, just sign me up for whatever is cheapest." Another meal spent with the sales team from Dakota Telecom.

So, clearly Sprint had a great idea, which was to simplify long-distance savings. They called this idea SprintSense—their new Valuable Formula. If they call you some evening offering you, a competitor's customer, their rate-savings package, and you ask them, "What is SprintSense?" they'll tell you, "10 cents a minute." Is that a clear statement of focus? Yes. Is that a Valuable Formula that makes sense and appeals to the customer? Yes. We all like paying lower rates, and we like knowing what those rates are without having to tabulate them. Meanwhile, we can still anticipate another call soon from Dakota Telecom with some other plan. Thanks to Sprint, we can just hang up the phone and get back to dinner.

Is this a Valuable Formula? Anyone who makes long-distance calls would say so. Even more indicative is the fact that in the months following the birth of SprintSense, Sprint gained market share in every one of them. In essence, Sprint has run through all three phases of the growth cycle. It has created, exploited, transitioned, created, and has entered the high-value exploit phase once again.

Now let's use the long-distance telephone market to illustrate the Valuable Formula and bring it to life. Observe that in Figure 4.3 we have isolated each of the aspects of the SprintSense Valuable Formula, from the focal hub to the outlying supports comprising the market proposition and the business system. Sprint has a focus: to simplify long-distance savings. It met an important, unsatisfied customer need. For this, the company established a low price of 10 cents a minute. They were able to set that low rate because of their low operating costs. Sprint found that most consumers make their personal phone calls during their social hours—in the evenings and on weekends. Due to their strong base of business customers, Sprint's calling volume was heaviest when business callers made their phone calls, between 7 a.m. and 7 p.m. So, there was low volume or "excess capacity" in the optimal time slots for consumer long-distance activity. Thus, their effective costs were low enough to support the 10 cents a minute price and still be value creating for Sprint. As the figure shows, this excellent "price/value" relationship in the market proposition that the customer sees exists because their "operations" in their business system, which are not seen by customers, were in proper alignment. Further, their service and support systems were so well-established that they have won an award for the plan's high quality from J. D. Power and Associates[5] for four consecutive years.

During the create phase, Sprint realized it had these supportive structures working for it. The company realized it had a Valuable Formula. Look at the "competitive position" spoke on the market proposition half of the figure. With AT&T tied into its "True Savings" plan and MCI equally locked into its "Friends & Family" rate package, Sprint had pioneered a customer-service innovation for the industry. They were well ahead of the pack, allowing plenty of leverage to exploit it. We are all familiar with Candice Bergen, "the

Sprint—From "Pin Drop" to SprintSense

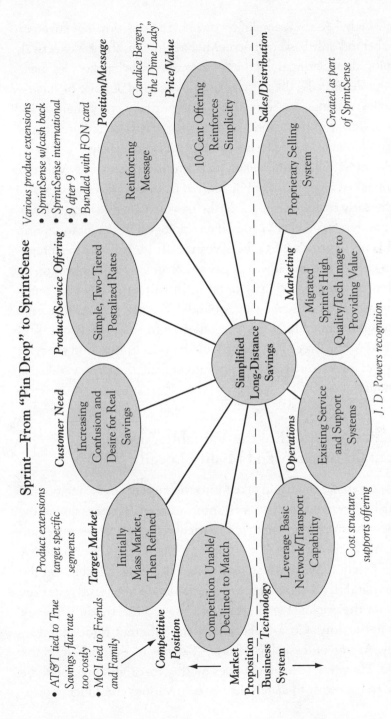

Figure 4.3. Sprint's Valuable Formula.

Dime Lady." As the second most recognizable advertising spokesperson, behind only basketball icon Michael Jordan, she was effectively employed for Sprint along the "position/message" spoke. Customers saw her reinforcing the message of Sprint's basic promise of value—simplified savings—in television ads on virtually every channel and in a majority of time slots. With a clear, easily articulated focus, Sprint was able to stop losing the long-distance battle.

In mid-1998, Sprint began once again to re-create its Valuable Formula. At the time of publication of this book, its efforts are still in the early stages. Sprint ION,[6] the newest Valuable Formula, represents thus far about a $2 billion technology investment for Sprint. Bill Esrey, Sprint's CEO, believes it will be yet another breakthrough. For the user it will satisfy a yearning for even lower prices and increased productivity. For Sprint it will mean lowering transport costs even further, by an astounding 70 percent! At its core is something termed ION, an Integrated On-demand Network. Will it work? We will see. True to the growth cycle, Sprint is on the right strategic track, managing its transition and creating a new Valuable Formula.

Practice 6: Globalize the Valuable Formula; Maintain Integrity and Modify Locally

Once created, tested, and taken into the market in one region, the Valuable Formula can be taken international. There is a seeming paradox with this practice. It is critical to retain the essence and integrity of the formula as it is taken global or it will become a new and different formula, which may or may not be as valuable. On the other hand, if all elements of the formula are kept *exactly* as they were for the original region, the chances are small that it will work in other regions. Coca-Cola bridges the inherent trade-off effectively. As one of their slogans says, "Coke is it" everywhere in the world. However, Coca-Cola does modify its original recipe to be more or less sweet to match the tastes of various consumer populations. Thus, Coke maintains the integrity of its U.S.-born product while increasing its appeal for the Asian, European, and South American markets.

Another example is Starbucks, which faces a similar challenge when taking its Seattle-based coffee bar to the world market. The corner Starbucks near our office in Boston is officially and assertively nonsmoking. In Boston nonsmoking is de rigueur and legally mandated. But can Starbucks succeed in France where smoking is de rigueur? How important is the smoking/non-smoking element to Starbucks' Valuable Formula? Starbucks must answer this query as it expands globally.

An excellent current object lesson in globalization of a Valuable Formula is the magazine *Men's Health*. Founded a decade ago[7] to provide "tons of useful stuff" to U.S. males, the magazine has been a phenomenal success. It has found a niche speaking on issues of men's health, fitness, and active lifestyles (including sexuality). The magazine's explosive growth in the United States gave its editor, Mike Lafavore, and its publisher, Jeff Morgan, the confidence to try global editions. They carefully plotted an international growth agenda, selecting which markets to attack and in what order. To limit the number of variables, they decided to try Anglo-Saxon countries and countries of scale first. They made another smart strategic decision, to build *Men's Health* into a global brand that just happened to have a large, domestic U.S. market. All editions (about a dozen to date) use a black-and-white cover, have a shirtless male on the cover, and use the English language title *Men's Health* across the top. All editions look, feel, and read like the same magazine. But they also have a local flavor. For instance, the Russian edition has a Russian subtitle (rough translation: "The Man Himself") with a macho connotation and using the Cyrillic alphabet. In the Americas, the ideal male body image is a well-defined, chiseled physique with a prominently etched "six pack" of abdominal muscles. In Germany, a decidedly "beefier" male is the ideal. In the United States, where readers have a relatively high disposable income, articles feature workouts in the gym and with expensive in-home equipment. In Russia, with a lower level of disposable income, articles describe exercise routines that can be done at home or with simple, inexpensive equipment. Thus, each country's edition is a local modification of the magazine's basic Valuable Formula. *Men's Health* is well on its way to building global brand recognition.

Practice 7: Leverage Two Key Strategic Weapons— Innovation and Alliances—to Exploit Valuable Formulas

As we have worked with and researched growth companies, we have found that they leverage their Valuable Formulas by using two strategic weapons extensively, namely *innovation* and *alliances*. Innovation is fairly obvious. Fast-growing companies bring new products and services to their customers up to twice as fast as other companies. They set high new-product development goals. They invest heavily. Further, they design, build, and monitor effective innovation processes. In fact, companies such as Corning, the 1997 Malcolm Baldrige winner for innovation, win awards for their prowess. We all expect high-growth companies to be paradigms of innovation.

However, our discovery of the aggressive use of alliances by high-growth companies was more surprising. After all, growth companies create value, and most research suggests that alliances have high failure rates. In conjunction with our book, *Teaming Up for the '90s*,[8] we conducted a global survey on the alliance experience. We collected information on nearly five hundred transactions[9] and found that experience could be an excellent teacher. That is, inexperienced companies (those with fewer than three alliances) had a failure rate approaching 90 percent. In contrast, experienced companies (companies with more than ten alliances) had a success rate of about 75 percent. By sharing learning from one transaction to another, a company builds a universe of "best practices," improving the odds for each succeeding transaction. In further research, we analyzed a set of the twenty-five most active alliance-forming companies within the Fortune 500. These alliance activists have a three-year return to their investors a full 50 percent higher than the average of all other companies. However, the variance in performance was also higher, underscoring the value of and the need for learning. Mere repetition does not improve the aptitude for alliances—only knowledge does. *The Alliance Analyst*,[10] the leading journal in the alliance field, performed its own analysis, which confirmed our theory. Use alliances aggressively, but learn to use them effectively.

Globalization is a natural rationale for forming alliances. *Men's Health*'s Jeff Morgan describes himself as an "alliance junkie." In each market entered, he has forged a relationship to access highly country-specific distribution networks. Starbucks formed an alliance in Japan with Sazerby, which has helped them by providing local market input to mold its Seattle-style coffeehouse Valuable Formula to Japanese tastes.

Given what you have learned in this chapter, ask yourself the following questions: Is our Valuable Formula focused, and does it feature a distinctive market proposition and a well-formed business system? Next fill out the Growth Strategy Scorecard in Exhibit 4.1.

Make sure your formula embodies a clear goal and a coherent message to the marketplace and the organization. The Valuable Formula model is a particularly effective tool for mapping and measuring your progress. Because the model is divided into the market proposition and the business system and has many branches, you can chart exactly where your competition is affecting your progress. Is it somewhere that counts, such as price/value? If so, you must decide whether or not to fine-tune your formula or scrap it altogether. Or you may want to continue exploiting your formula.

Another reason why the model is useful is to find your connections with the customers. We saw in the case of SprintSense that Candice Bergen has had no trouble communicating the value in the

Practice 4:
Create a Valuable Formula as a Platform
for Long-Term Growth

- Do you have a clear focus?
- Is your market proposition responsive to customers and competitively superior?
- Is your business system coherent with the other elements of your formula?

Practice 5:
Manage the Valuable Formula Across the Growth Cycle

- Do you monitor challenges to the Valuable Formula?
- Do you employ separate measurement tools to gauge which growth phase the Valuable Formula is in?
- Have you designed distinct processes and/or identified different teams to manage during the three growth phases?

Practice 6:
Globalize the Valuable Formula; Maintain Integrity
and Modify Locally

- Can you identify which elements must be modified locally?
- Are you truly building a global brand?

Practice 7:
Leverage Two Key Strategic Weapons—
Innovation and Alliances—to Exploit Valuable Formulas

- How well-developed are your innovation and alliance processes?
- Do you actively leverage these processes across divisions? Globally?

Exhibit 4.1. Growth Strategy Scorecard.

Sprint formula to the marketplace. If it's easy for customers to understand, and your market proposition and business systems are coherent and supportive, you will have created a Valuable Formula. Your company will grow. Next you must build your foundations to sustain that growth.

5

Growth Capability

How to Build the Foundations for Sustained Growth

Our third cornerstone, *capability*, completes the structure of the Growth System. This cornerstone enables the enterprise to sustain value-creating growth well into the future, far beyond the transitory trendy product or charismatic leader. We know all hot ideas cool off eventually. We also know all leaders eventually retire. But the enterprise can survive, thrive, and grow. Strong, well-aligned foundations carry the enterprise forward. We have found, from working with high-performance, high-growth companies, such as Hewlett-Packard, Rodale, Parexel, and General Electric, that capability for the business to carry on is embedded in five growth-supporting foundations: leadership, architecture, culture, processes, and knowledge. The salient attributes of these foundations are shown in Figure 5.1.[1]

Average companies differ in that they have not embedded such growth-supporting foundations. Whatever transitory success they achieve does not result in long-term revenue growth. For example, they may stop growing if a particularly insightful CEO steps down, if early growth and expansion into new markets lead to losses in profit and market share, or if globalization slows their ability to communicate internal knowledge throughout far-flung offices. Long-term growers have these supporting foundations in place.

FOUNDATION	DIFFERENTIATING ATTRIBUTES
Leadership	• Believable, deeply committed growth vision • Strong leader development programs • Drive for market dominance • Understanding of where value is created
Architecture	• Focus on core competencies —Invest in them, organize around them, leverage them across businesses •Tight performance metrics • Team structures
Culture	• Vision with defined goals communicated • Close to the customer • Norms and structures that foster teamwork • Very demanding yet very rewarding
Processes	• Well-developed innovation process —In place and structured, with highly defined metrics • Effective alliance development process • Critical growth processes identified and redesigned
Knowledge	• Customer information/communication • Intellectual capital leveraged • Broad shareholder information sharing

Figure 5.1. Attributes That Distinguish High-Growth Companies.

Although it is obvious, it is important to note that, by definition and by their nature, successful growth companies will continue to grow. They will discover new products and target customers; they will become large companies with many bases of operation; and they will become national, then global. It is ironic that the biggest challenges for growth companies are those brought on by growth itself. Growth stretches an organization into areas and situations for which it has not had experience. Without growth-supporting foundations, an expanding company will crumble on itself. It is essential to project and provide for the growth you strive to achieve.

Practice 8: Identify and Nurture
All Growth-Supporting Processes

As a precursor to strengthening the five foundations shown in Figure 5.1, we recommend that companies first develop a process map. We call this an "industry print," a tool to identify operational and support processes for a company's key businesses. After creating the process map, an organization's next step is to isolate those processes and subprocesses central to driving growth so that it can decide which need special attention or, during efforts at cost reduction, the organization can keep the growth drivers intact. Remember that even if you are suffering through a business slump, you must grow again to create value for stakeholders. Do not hamstring your ability to build future revenue by decimating a process critical for growth. Figure 5.2 is an example of an "industry print"[2]—a high-level process map for a high-tech manufacturing company.

An example of adhering to the principle of protecting those processes critical for growth is one client company CEO's statement in 1994 when the company was experiencing the need for cost reduction. He said: "For this effort to succeed, there must be no 'sacred cows,' no issues too emotional to address. By the way, there is a second guideline for you to bear in mind as a certainty. Do not touch, do not even breathe on, Research Park. It will not be part of this process redesign."

Research Park is the core of their innovation process. The company is demanding of this process and facility to generate new products on a continual, rapid cycle. Although its companywide operating costs are high, its innovation rate is admired by all. But was the CEO saying that their innovation process was perfect? Did he believe that nothing should change? Of course not. Rather, he understood the company's growth-supporting processes and was ensuring that the R&D at the core of its success was to be protected from any cost-cutting zeal. In fact, eighteen months later, at the tail

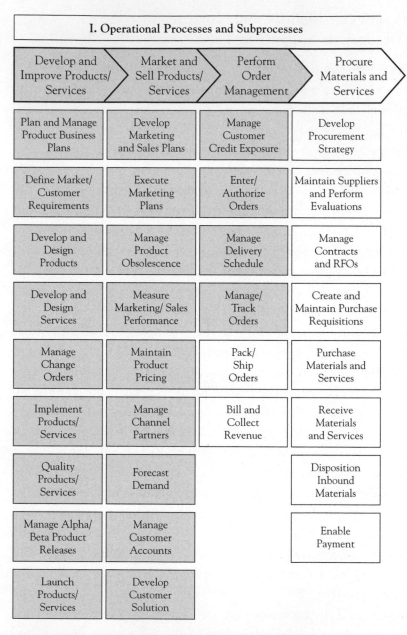

I. Operational Processes and Subprocesses

Develop and Improve Products/ Services	Market and Sell Products/ Services	Perform Order Management	Procure Materials and Services
Plan and Manage Product Business Plans	Develop Marketing and Sales Plans	Manage Customer Credit Exposure	Develop Procurement Strategy
Define Market/ Customer Requirements	Execute Marketing Plans	Enter/ Authorize Orders	Maintain Suppliers and Perform Evaluations
Develop and Design Products	Manage Product Obsolescence	Manage Delivery Schedule	Manage Contracts and RFOs
Develop and Design Services	Measure Marketing/ Sales Performance	Manage/ Track Orders	Create and Maintain Purchase Requisitions
Manage Change Orders	Maintain Product Pricing	Pack/ Ship Orders	Purchase Materials and Services
Implement Products/ Services	Manage Channel Partners	Bill and Collect Revenue	Receive Materials and Services
Quality Products/ Services	Forecast Demand		Disposition Inbound Materials
Manage Alpha/ Beta Product Releases	Manage Customer Accounts		Enable Payment
Launch Products/ Services	Develop Customer Solution		

Growth process: an operational or support process that is a primary revenue driver

Figure 5.2. Example of an "Industry Print" for a High-Tech Company.

I. Operational Processes and Subprocesses

Manufacture Products	Manage Logistics	Provide Customer Services
Define Manufacturing Strategy	Develop Distributor and Logistics Strategy	Manage Service Delivery
Manage Manufacturing Operations	Determine Material Handling Strategy	Provide Internal and External Training
Plan Production (Sales/Ops Planning)	Receive Material (Non-Supplier)	Provide Single Point of Contact
Schedule Production (MPS/MPR)	Manage Inventory Storage and Movement	Exchange/ Return Products
Execute Production	Manage Import/ Export	Perform Phone Support
Disposition Products		Provide Field Installation/ Service
Manage Line Replenishment		Perform System Repair
Report Production Operations Efficiency		Provide Consulting Services

Key

Growth Processes	Support Processes

II. Infrastructure Processes and Subprocesses			
Plan and Manage Business	Perform Financial and Managerial Accounting	Manage Human Resources	Manage Information Resources
Define Business Strategy and Plan	Manage the General Ledger	Plan and Organize Human Resources	Define and Plan Information Resource Needs
Manage Business Performance	Plan and Manage Taxes	Manage Vacancy to New Hire Assimilation	Formulate the IT Strategy
Plan Business	Manage Fixed Assets	Develop and Train Workforce	Develop and Enhance the Data Architecture/ Software Application
Improve Business Performance	Manage Treasury Activities	Manage Workforce	Develop and Enhance Infrastructure and Interface
Plan and Manage Quality Performance	Perform Overhead Accounting	Manage Payroll	Manage Information Systems Operations
	Manage Product Costing	Manage Rewards	Provide Information User Support
	Perform Profitability Analysis	Manage Employee Benefits	
	Coordinate/ Perform Audit		
	Perform Closing		
	Report and Analyze Performance		

Figure 5.2. Continued.

II. Infrastructure Processes and Subprocesses

Manage Plant Maintenance	Manage Capital Projects	Manage Support Services
Maintain Plant Maintenance Data and Documentation	Develop Project Alternatives and Analyze Feasibility	Manage Administrative Services
Identify and Plan Plant Maintenance	Plan Project	Manage Corporate Communication
Schedule Plant Maintenance	Schedule Project	Ensure Employee Communications
Execute Plant Maintenance	Execute Project	Provide Legal Services
Root Cause Analysis		Plan and Manage Environmental/ Safety Programs
		Risk Management

Key

Growth Processes

Support Processes

end of the reengineering program, Research Park was itself analyzed and redesigned to improve its world-class processes. This company generated nearly $10 billion in revenue in 1998 and continues to grow.

Practice 9: Benchmark Your Growth Foundations vs. the "Best of the Best" and Aim to Beat Them

Each foundation of the Growth System is essential. Although your organization might become a high performer without mastering all of them, by enhancing your skill at every one, you can increase your chances of achieving long-term growth. As you will do with the other two cornerstones, you will need to keep a scorecard on your company's five capability foundations in order to evaluate your progress continually. Correct your weaknesses and capitalize on your strengths. Don't wait for failure to get your attention; make sure the following foundations are in place while you are executing the growth cycle. If they are, you will grow—and be prepared to grow more.

Leadership

Leadership is not just who a company's leaders are today, but rather comprises the company's ability to build tomorrow's leaders, to communicate a growth vision to employees, and to keep the vision from one generation of leadership to the next. Leaders don't just pen the growth vision, they teach their employees to draw it themselves. Everyone in such a company understands that growth is critical and is deeply committed to it. Strong leadership means inspiring people to look for breakthrough opportunities, as well as incremental product development that will lead to market dominance. Most importantly, it means establishing leadership development and counseling programs to ensure that there is an equally committed, emerging generation of leaders that understands where value is created.

As a paradigm of leadership, General Electric can be our benchmark. We have helped teach their Business Management Course, which consists of young, high-talent people in mid-career, about growth. (Incidentally, this program also shows the commitment GE has made to growth.) GE's CEO, Jack Welch, decided to train these future executives to be world-class leaders and to learn the importance of growth in the future. He molded his young leaders for two years before he announced to the world that GE intended to be the first $70 billion growth company.[3] When he made his proclamation, he already had one hundred people in place to pursue his vision.

Architecture

The next foundation, *architecture*, is best described by our friend and colleague, Brian Quinn,[4] professor emeritus at Dartmouth's Amos Tuck School of Business. When he speaks of a company's architecture, he poses the question, "Have you created an intelligent enterprise?" By that he means a company that knows itself, its personality, and its character. To have a strong architecture, a company must truly understand its core competencies, must strive to make them world-class, and must leverage them to their fullest advantage. Does your organization invest in its core competencies by researching and supporting them? Can you leverage these competencies across diverse businesses? Further, have you aligned your performance incentives with your organization's growth goals by rewarding those people and departments who help you meet your growth target or open new businesses? Your company should be designed and organized to deploy its competencies efficiently and expertly, to take its growth plans and Valuable Formulas into the market early and often to achieve the maximum advantage.

Following are two examples of intelligent enterprises: One has come to fruition and one still aspires. Boeing redefined itself between the launch of its successful 747 and its new 777. The company stretched itself almost to its breaking point as it developed and built the 747 largely on its own. For the 777, its approach shifted radically. Whereas 70 percent of the value added to the 747 was Boeing's, barely 30 percent of the value added to the 777 was internal;

the remainder was provided by an advanced network of effective supplier alliances that allowed Boeing to focus on its strengths as prime designer and systems integrator. This alliance-based approach to focusing on core competencies, along with tight performance metrics and team structures, makes Boeing best in its class in this growth foundation.

Ford's "Ford 2000"[5] initiative is another example of a new vision for a company's architecture. Ford has reinforced its long-term goal to be a global enterprise and plans to restructure around a series of design and product development centers around the globe. Each center will have a focus, for example, trucks, small cars, or large cars, and each will be responsible for designing a particular type of product for sale globally. Ford 2000 is still a vision, but a good example of the role of architecture as a critical foundation for growth.

Culture

The third foundation is a growth-oriented *culture*. Any company that has been in business for more than five years is likely to have a well-defined culture. Whether or not it is a growth-inspired or growth-driven culture will determine the organization's success. Growth-oriented organizations have norms that foster teamwork. Group meetings, cooperation, and shared information predominate. Communication is accomplished across functions, businesses, and geographies within such companies; there is no limit to their concept of "teamwork." Another cultural aspect is a strong predisposition toward using customer needs to drive internal decision making and internal processes. Again, boundaries between client and company response are ignored.

Furthermore, fast-growing companies both demand more and reward more than slow growers. Because employees at high-growth companies are under intense pressure, they tend to be motivated by rewards beyond the thrill and opportunity that growth itself provides. Critical to striking a balance between high intensity and liberal reward is to ensure that those who perform well (often teams of people) are recognized and rewarded. As a company increases in size, it becomes impossible to observe performance directly, so formal systems are built to replace firsthand knowledge about performance. If formal systems cannot keep pace with actual performance, the company-employee compact can break down. Intensity wears down people who are not given proper levels of reward and recognition, and the company becomes political, not performance oriented. Political companies are anti-growth; they develop slow-growth DNA.

Rodale Press, the world's largest health and fitness publisher, provides an excellent example of a growth culture with its "tree" icon, shown in Figure 5.3.[6] Rodale does not so much encourage teamwork as demand it. Its vision and commitment are so well articulated and deeply understood that virtually every employee begins a description of the company and its values the same way. The company uses a picture of a tree showing both its above-ground beauty—the foliage, representing products for customers—and its below-ground fortitude—the root system, representing the people and values core to its continuing success. Bob Rodale, the company's second-generation CEO, designed this symbol and icon. As a leader, he was as central to Rodale's success as Bill Gates is to Microsoft's. Although Rodale passed away tragically in 1991, the company has continued to grow, to create new products, and to expand internationally. Why? Because Bob's legacy, embodied in the tree, is the growth culture he created, in fact, the full panoply of growth-supporting foundations. Thus, not only is the tree symbol pervasive in the consciousness of the corporation, but the symbol itself traces the interlocking efforts that distinguish the Rodale company culture. Bob Rodale's successor, Bob Teufel, a thirty-year company veteran, carries on the Rodale culture even though he is not a family member. The tree icon guides him as much as it did Bob Rodale.

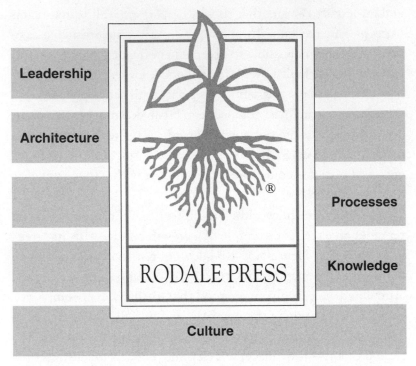

Figure 5.3. Rodale Press Logo Illustrating a Growth Culture.

Processes

The fourth foundation is the *processes* a company establishes to implement its ideas. Obviously the innovation and alliance processes are critical to growth, but successful growth companies pay very close attention to *all* of their critical growth-oriented processes, both to creating them and to refurbishing them. Our definition of "processes" comes from our work with Dr. Michael Hammer. He describes a process as "the complete end-to-end set of activities that create value for the customer." These include both internal-support activities, such as business planning or team training and development, and customer-support activities, such as customer service or new product development. For example, the "innovation" process threads through the entire Growth System, bridging the gap between the "create" and "exploit" phases as new products are fine-tuned and then ensuring that there are adequate resources and a strong commitment to capture the product's full potential.

Corning, the recent winner of the Malcolm Baldrige award for best-in-the-world innovation, is an exemplar of a strong innovation process during the create phase of the growth cycle.

Knowledge

Companies that grow successfully communicate their best practices to the rest of the organization almost immediately. Such shared *knowledge* is essential both for understanding and communicating a company's commitment to growth and for putting it into action. An idea spawned in the Chicago office should be in the hands of the Sydney staff by the next morning, and so on. In addition, successful high-growth companies leverage their intellectual capital and share information widely with all stakeholders. *The Power of Corporate Kinetics*, a recent book by Mike Fradette and Steve Michaud,[7] describes companies that are adept at sharing their knowledge.

Actually, our studies have turned up an interesting fact concerning exchange of information. We found that companies that transferred information best had very high travel and entertainment expenses. We learned that technology—in the form of intranets, teleconferencing, or courier services—was often insufficient for communicating learning. Successful growers travel. They board a plane to see people at their satellite locations, spending significant time and money going places to spread knowledge. The lesson to be learned is to use technology, but not to let its limitations slow the sharing of ideas. Remember that fast growers meet their cohorts face-to-face.

Takeaway

Fast growers meet their cohorts face-to-face. They share
knowledge beyond technological limitations.

Hewlett-Packard provides the benchmark for the knowledge foundation, which is not surprising given the fact that HP's business is based on information and systems that support its use. Shared knowledge is essential for HP and for all companies because a Valuable Formula could easily come from any one of an organization's far-flung offices. Good concepts must be circulated quickly so that processes can be put into place to deliver products or services to customers, increasing revenue and shareholder value.

Best in Class

To further illustrate the five foundations, we have drawn a table of familiar names that represent the "best in class" for each. For each U.S. company in Table 5.1, we have listed a global category equivalent. All of these companies provide the best possible benchmarks for their respective foundations.

Practice 10: Design and Implement Initiatives to Align Foundations

As we discussed earlier, the concept of Ford 2000, a quintessential growth-driven initiative, is aimed at making a $150 billion company into a truly global enterprise. Ford aims to make not a small car in the United States that's built for Europe, but a small car in Europe that's built for the world. The organization is trying to do so with a new *architecture* in place.

In the *culture* category, Asahi recently overtook Kirin by growing at a rate of 10 percent in the Japanese beer industry, which grew at just 1 percent during the same period. Asahi did it not through price competition, but by unleashing its growth culture.

Table 5.1. Growth Foundation Benchmark Companies and Their Exceptional Strengths.

Foundation	U.S. Example	Global Example
Leadership	GE	Carrefour (France)
Architecture	Boeing	Village Roadshow (Australia)
Culture	Rodale Press	Asahi Beer (Japan)
Process	Corning	Mitsubishi Trading (Japan)
Knowledge	Hewlett-Packard	Nissan (Japan)

Carrefour has set an aggressive *leadership* tone, one that perhaps would not be accepted as well here in the United States as it is in France. Their pledge is, "Whatever market we get into, we're going to dominate." Dominate—not lead, but dominate. Employees know that each time they enter a new market that they must find a way to vanquish it.

As we expected, our research showed that high-growth companies differ sharply from their low-growth counterparts on the five foundations. Figure 5.4 shows the graphs for both in all foundations. The high-growth companies, those growing above 15 percent annually, are pictured at the top and those growing at less than 5 percent per year appear at the bottom of each graph.

Working with these high-caliber organizations, we found that we could define each of the foundations by breaking it into roughly twenty characteristics. The characteristics being compared appear at the bottom of the graph for leadership. Attributes for the other foundations were defined in similar fashion.[8]

The scores themselves are based on thousands of surveys and personal interviews with our numerous "benchmark partners," as discussed in Chapter Two.[9] We found wide variances between high-growth and low-growth organizations across factor after factor, as shown in Figure 5.4.

You might use this type of graph to guide your own behavior. To illustrate, we'll use the graph of an anonymous client we'll call

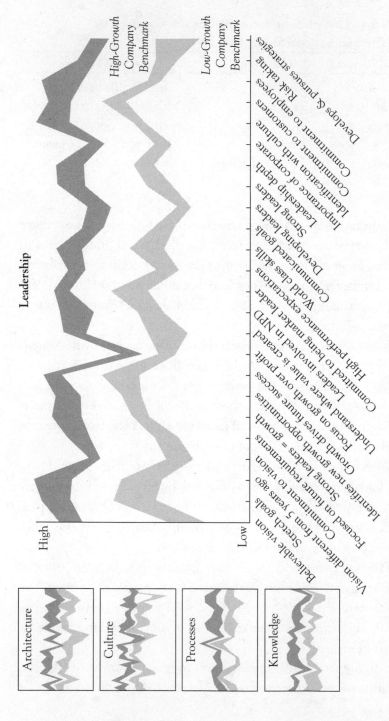

Figure 5.4. High-Growth Versus Low-Growth Company Foundations.

"Silicon Valley High-Flyer."[10] The company's graph is about two years old. Figure 5.5 shows their "culture foundation" (the dotted line) plotted against the high-grower benchmark (the top band). It is obvious that although the company was growing at about 50 percent per year at the time, their culture was not close to the high-growth benchmark. We predicted they would have trouble sustaining their growth.

Interestingly, the High-Flyer's culture looked remarkably similar to that of a Boston area high-growth company. Both faced emerging cultural shortcomings. The Boston company had realized that rapid expansion had caused its culture to get out of sync. That company's CEO recognized the reason for the company's deteriorating cultural foundation, namely that the company had changed immensely since its inception. Everyone used to work in the same building, but now the company had operations in various cities; everyone used to be in the United States, now half the employees were in Europe. He had personally hired everyone in the beginning, and now there were people working for him whom he did not know at all, some having joined the company through acquisitions. As a result, the culture had become diluted. To correct the problem, he decided to increase his travel and entertainment budget. He created what he called the "Renew the Growth Culture Initiative" and went out to talk to all the employees in different places, articulating the culture he desired for the company. When we had identified the cultural deficiency, the company was operating at 35 percent growth per year. Today, the company maintains that 35 percent annual revenue growth. Its culture profile has now come back in line with its original vision, consistent with the company's high-growth peers. This company's CEO recognized a shortcoming and then designed and implemented an effective solution.

To return to the Silicon Valley High-Flyer, the company's growth rate was around 50 percent when we identified the problem. We gave them similar advice: Take action to spread the cultural message. They had a very different reaction. The CEO thought (in

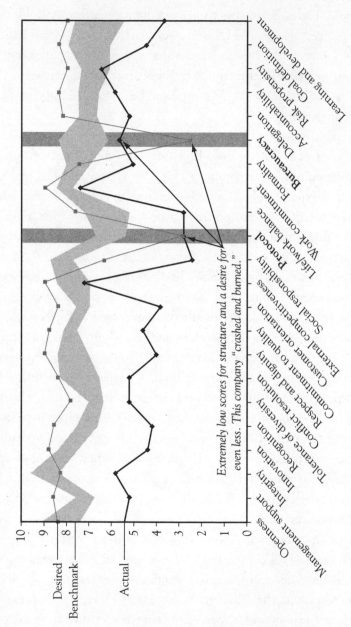

Sample Comparison of Culture Foundation

Extremely low scores for structure and a desire for even less. This company "crashed and burned."

Figure 5.5. Comparison of a Company's Culture Foundation with the Benchmark.

polite paraphrase) that our concept of his company's culture was bunk and that our advice was soft, off-target, and irrelevant. Unfortunately, fifteen months later, their final quarterly revenue registered at 0 percent growth. We were surprised that their growth hit the wall quite so quickly. However, we were not surprised at all that it failed. Growth-supporting foundations sustain growth. Weakened foundations do not. Unlike their Massachusetts counterpart, whose CEO identified a problem and went on the road to realign his cultural foundation, the Silicon Valley company chose not to do so.

The High-Flyer made a mistake that many fast-growing companies make. It did not take care of its foundations. The High-Flyer did not do what it takes to sustain growth. It is possible to grow too fast. The High-Flyer grew faster than its foundations could sustain. As we saw in Figure 1.4 in Chapter One, not all growth is good. Sometimes growth can destroy value, and sometimes success can mask inadequacies. The first problem comes from inadequate financial returns; the second results from neglected foundations.

Again, we come to a scorecard. Measure yourself on Exhibit 5.1 in each of the growth capability categories against the benchmark partners or against a high-performance peer or competitor.

With the characteristics of the five growth-supporting foundations outlined in this chapter, we finished mapping the principles of the Growth System: commitment, strategy, and capability. The key to understanding the system is to see the unifying and cyclical nature of it, as shown by the growth cycle model earlier. No one piece can be the sole focus of your attention. The Growth System is a complex framework that cycles continually. Only by understanding this interconnectedness, this holistic approach to growth, will your company gain the high-performance advantages of growth. Keeping the system in mind will help your organization to reach Nirvana—when growth will become the process that delivers sustainable value to shareholders, customers, employees, and

---

Practice 8:
Identify and Nurture All Growth-Supporting Processes

- Can you list and show graphically linkages between all of your operational and infrastructure processes?

- Have you designated processes that drive growth? If so, are they given special consideration during cost-reduction efforts?

Practice 9:
Benchmark Growth Foundations vs. the "Best of the Best" and Aim to Beat Them

- Have you researched a group of companies you can relate to that are "the best" in each foundation?

- How do you measure up?

Practice 10:
Design and Implement Initiatives to Align Foundations

- What initiatives have you set in motion to leverage your strengths?

- What initiatives have you chartered to overcome key foundation weaknesses?

Exhibit 5.1. Growth Capability Scorecard.

the economy—everywhere that matters. Next we come to Part II, in which you will learn how to align your company so that it can reach the destination.

Part II

Reaching the Destination

Aligning the Enterprise

Beginning the Journey

Now we move to the second stage of our journey toward value-creating growth: aligning the enterprise. We began by listing and describing the basic practices an organization must follow to grow successfully. In this second stage, we help you understand:

- Whether or not you have the basics in place; and

- If not, how to make the changes necessary to align with the model of successful growth.

Several key themes course through this stage. First, *it is essential to prepare properly and act effectively.* Second, *growth is a learned competence, any and all can learn how to do it.* Third, *understanding the Growth System model and applying it to your own enterprise will allow you to develop the required growth competency.* Recall that the model was developed by examining how other companies have achieved and sustained value-creating growth. Finally, *the path to growth is a never-ending journey, rather than a destination.* As we learned from examining the growth cycles of successful fast-growing organizations, we must be dynamic and we must keep moving.

In this second stage, we'll show how to diagnose your fitness for the journey and how to put into practice the lessons learned from the successful growth companies.

6

The Growth Diagnostic
Your Growth Fitness

A n enterprise with a well-developed Growth System, one with all of its cornerstones properly aligned, is ready and will be able to unleash the power of growth. Especially as organizations increase in size and complexity, they must have the gears of their growth engines oiled well. In this chapter, you will learn how to test your own company to see whether the gears (cornerstones) are aligned. Further, you will learn how to both diagnose and correct problems as they come up.

In Figure 6.1, we list ten "essential practices" embedded in the Growth System's cornerstones. Each of these practices can be tested to ensure that an enterprise is in alignment. We test whether an organization believes in, articulates, and establishes a *commitment* to growth. We test whether an organization is able to create, manage, globalize, and leverage a growth *strategy*; and we test an organization's *capabilities* by its ability to identify growth-critical processes, benchmark against superior performance, and design systems to grow.

The three tests are designed to compare "best practices" of your company against best practices of a successful high-growth company. This approach is depicted graphically in Figure 6.2. Essentially, you will take an inventory of your company's actual growth-oriented actions, practices, and processes from the inside out. You then compare and contrast these actions, practices, and processes with our

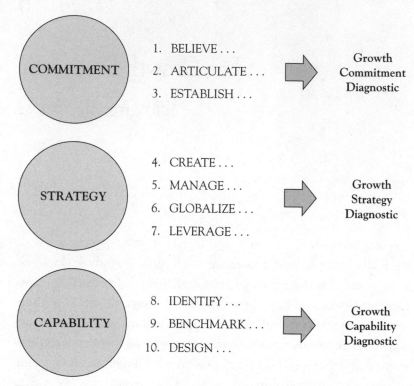

Figure 6.1. Ten Essential Practices Drive an Effective Diagnosis.

model of a successful growth company from the outside in. We call this the *growth diagnostic*, which usually offers great insight and helps to achieve the following key objectives to:

- Determine where you are or are not aligned

- Determine your growth potential

- Pinpoint problem areas

- Build consensus around issues

- Set priorities for initiatives to correct problems

By using the growth diagnostic as a model, you will be able to perform a rigorous analysis of your own organization in comparison

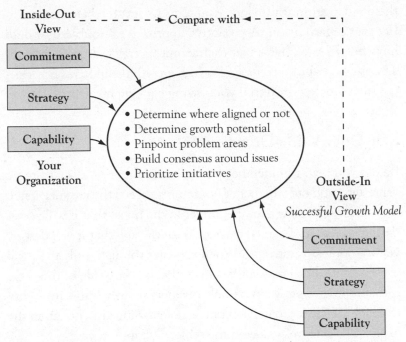

Figure 6.2. The Growth Diagnostic: Comparing an Organization with the Model of a Successful Grower.

with a successful fast-growing organization. Such a comparison will help to shift the focus inside your organization from a debate about how to find out what the problems are to where and how to improve.

We prescribe the growth diagnostic to both ailing and healthy companies. It helps organizations not only to repair systems, but also to maintain them. Our recommendation is that all companies undergo periodic, comprehensive growth diagnoses to see whether sound growth systems are in place. If your company is showing no signs of revenue growth, the decision about whether to apply the diagnostic and repair your diseased growth principles is obvious. But even if your company is currently achieving the high-performance value results signifying successful growth, take the test. As the Silicon Valley High-Flyer we described in Chapter Five demonstrated, there is danger in waiting for symptoms to develop before examining your organization. A proactive approach undoubtedly would have helped the High-Flyer to preempt its tragic drop in growth. This is our goal in recommending the growth diagnostic. The various steps are described in the following paragraphs.

Step One: Value-Growth Analysis

Before you begin, remember that growth does not always create value. First find out whether or not returns exceed the cost of capital. If you choose to grow a low performer in the hopes that it will power through the cost-of-capital barrier, do so realizing that it will destroy value as long as returns lag. When it breaks through, only then will it become a value creator. Of course, the opposite side of this issue is that failing to grow a profitable business sharply limits its ability to create value. A profitable business not growing fast enough in the exploit phase leaves value on the table, perhaps forever.

First you must analyze the value-creation potential of your company's various businesses. Place each business on the matrix shown in Figure 1.4 in Chapter One. Then follow the prescription for the quadrant the business is in. Although many business leaders seek to solve their problems by growing, often a lack of profitability is a signal that the business has not realized its *market proposition*. Or perhaps its *focus* is too broad, thus overwhelming its *business system*. In short, the business has not created a Valuable Formula. By temporarily reducing growth, even shrinking, such a business can recenter itself, uncover its Valuable Formula, and begin to exploit it by growing again.

Step Two: Phase Zero

After being sure that your value-growth prescriptions are in place, the challenge is to devote adequate time, resources, and personnel to diagnosing your company's fitness for growth. A dedicated task force should be established, made up of both senior-level and junior-level people who can devote at least 50 percent of their time to the growth diagnostic. When we say *at least* 50 percent of their time may be devoted to this analysis, we mean it is not unusual to devote 100 percent, but we try to be realistic about daily needs. Select talented people, not just the most available people. Having a variety of experience levels involved in the initiative is optimal, as senior members bring their broad perspective and deep experience and the newer employees bring their fresh, unique ideas. In tandem, the two groups work well. The effort should be scheduled to take six to eight weeks.

The diagnostic begins at what we call "phase zero," a preliminary two-day planning session at which the work plan is mapped out. Relevant questions at the session may include the following: "What are our existing growth goals?" "How much time will we devote to this analysis and when?" "What methods will we use to diagnose our fitness for growth?" "How will we collect data?"

To start, simply follow the prescriptions from the earlier chapters of this book. For example, you know you will compare your organization with the growth benchmark partners, your own competitors, or a peer group. Also, to help you begin, use the scorecards you have prepared on your company's practices. Exhibit 6.1 consolidates the three score cards from previous chapters for you.

Another way to analyze your organization is to use customer surveys, as your customers are one of the truest barometers of the effectiveness of your Valuable Formula. If you pool all your resources and concentrate time and effort, you will discover your unique keys to growth.

Figure 6.3 shows a work plan and typical timeline for a growth diagnostic. The diagnostic is intended to identify key preexisting strengths your company has for sustainable growth and also to flag areas of shortcoming or misalignment. It is analogous to an individual's annual physical: The physician tests the individual against a predetermined healthy model. If there are warning signals, the

Practice 1:
Believe Deeply That Growth Drives Value Creation

- Is the growth message understood and acted on at all levels, within all divisions and functions?

- Is growth an important agenda item at all management team meetings?

- Can you list specific actions being taken to drive growth?

Practice 2:
Articulate a Growth Vision; Embed It
Throughout the Organization

- Does a well-accepted statement exist underscoring the importance of growth?

- Do internal and external communications highlight growth efforts and results?

Practice 3:
Link Growth Performance to Rewards and Recognition

- Do formal measurement and reward systems explicitly incorporate growth? Are these systems understood?

- Are any symbolic awards tied to growth efforts and results?

Practice 4:
Create a Valuable Formula As a Platform for Long-Term Growth

- Do you have a clear focus?

- Is your market proposition responsive to customers and competitively superior?

Exhibit 6.1. Growth Commitment Scorecard.

- Is your business system coherent with the other elements of your formula?

Practice 5:
Manage the Valuable Formula Across the Growth Cycle

- Do you monitor challenges to the Valuable Formula?

- Do you employ separate measurement tools to gauge which growth phase the Valuable Formula is in?

- Have you designed distinct processes and/or identified different teams to manage during the three growth phases?

Practice 6:
Globalize the Valuable Formula; Maintain Integrity and Modify Locally

- Can you identify which elements must be modified locally?

- Are you truly building a global brand?

Practice 7:
Leverage Two Key Strategic Weapons—Innovation and Alliances—to Exploit Valuable Formulas

- How well-developed are your innovation and alliance processes?

- Do you actively leverage these processes across divisions? Globally?

Practice 8:
Identify and Nurture All Growth-Supporting Processes

- Can you list and show graphically linkages between all of your operational and infrastructure processes?

Exhibit 6.1. Continued.

- Have you designated processes that drive growth? If so, are they given special consideration during cost-reduction efforts?

Practice 9:
Benchmark Growth Foundations vs. the "Best of the Best"
and Aim to Beat Them

- Have you researched a group of companies you can relate to that are "the best" in each foundation?
- How do you measure up?

Practice 10:
Design and Implement Initiatives to Align Foundations

- What initiatives have you set in motion to leverage your strengths?
- What initiatives have you chartered to overcome key foundation weaknesses?

Exhibit 6.1. Continued.

next steps are to either take corrective action immediately or to test further to ensure accurate diagnosis. Similarly, applying the growth diagnostic identifies areas for immediate action or, if the signals are less clear, points out issues that require a closer look.

Step Three: Setting Expectations

You should expect one of two results from your growth diagnostic efforts. You may discover that you are significantly misaligned. Slow growth or a recent drop in growth may precede this discovery. In this case, the diagnostic will pinpoint where you have failed. With a clear vision of the obstacles that tripped you up, you can set priorities for overcoming them.

For slow growers, we recommend doing something early to spur growth in the short term. The short term? Yes, for growth is a

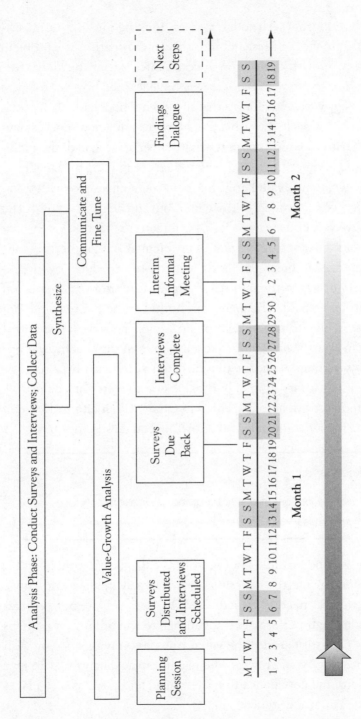

Figure 6.3. A Work Plan and Timeline for the Growth Diagnostic.

marathon journey. Although you are looking for long-term, sustainable growth, our research has shown that part of the problem with slow-growth or no-growth companies is that they have forgotten how to grow, and in fact may have learned how *not* to grow. An analogy we like to draw is that of a high school basketball coach we watched struggle through a trying first year at a new school. Having inherited a young but potentially superlative squad, the ambitious and energetic coach drew on years of playing and teaching experience, to no avail. Eerily, his team was competitive with every team it faced for much of the game, but in the final seconds the team always found a way to lose. As a matter of fact, it lost its first six games. Diagnosing his team's problem as one of inertia—not knowing how to break the losing legacy—he scheduled two weekend scrimmages in the mid-season against inferior opponents, off the win-loss record. The team won both. During the remainder of the season, the team won eight of ten games. The coach had taught the team how to win again. Take a lesson from the coach. Your priority after completing the diagnostic is to relearn how to grow immediately. Start simple, but make sure to start with a positive short-term growth activity. This will catalyze your efforts. Remember that if your company is not growing, you must jump-start it.

Takeaway

When your company is not growing, your first priority is to jump-start your growth engine *now*.

The second possible finding from the diagnostic could be that your company has the basics for growth largely in place and only a very few issues need to be addressed. Perhaps you are not yet realizing your high-performance advantage to the fullest. Or perhaps you are not satisfied with the value you are receiving and you wish to turbocharge your growth. The results of the diagnostic can give you additional confidence to move ahead and point you to places that need to be fine-tuned.

As a prospective guide for your own growth diagnostic, here are the ten issues we have uncovered as the most common growth-constraining shortcomings:

- Valuable Formulas are no longer working and cannot be leveraged across businesses.

- Competency is lacking in one or more of the growth phases, that is, create, exploit, or transition. (*Note:* If this is the problem, strategic alliance partners can help.)

- The business architecture constrains rapid deployment of new practices, products, and services.

- The two core growth processes—innovation and alliances—are missing or are underrepresented.

- Performance metrics are not aligned for growth nor linked to reward.

- The value/growth relationship is not concrete nor tied to reward.

- Key processes are not engineered for growth. (*Note:* Many companies cannot even identify their growth processes or do not protect them while restructuring or reengineering.)

- Information technology is not capable of supporting growth needs.

- Human resource models and systems are not aligned for growth.

- Although globalization looks promising, the company is not adequately prepared to grow into global markets.

Although each organization is by design and practice unique and each outcome of the growth diagnostic is unique to an organization, use the issues we've just listed as a checklist—a means of focusing your diagnostic efforts. In summary, the growth diagnostic is useful for companies that are not growing (obviously), as well as for those that *are* growing (not so obviously). The diagnostic is an effective tool for being proactive about growth. Do not emulate the High-Flyer. Remember the study we reported in the Introduction, which showed that only one in seven high-growth companies sustains high-level growth over fifteen years. Of the six that stumbled, only one in three was able to regain its momentum over the course of five years. These statistics alone should make you want to push hard for the promise of growth that creates value. This diagnostic has proved itself as a powerful *leading indicator* of a company's ability to reach that promise.

Step Four: The Analytical Process

Finding the source of an ailment is one thing. Effectively treating it is another. Whether your company comes up fit or failing, your next step is deciding what to do with the results. Because each cornerstone has its own set of basic practices, it is best to analyze each in turn (as we did with the scorecards). We have developed a series of questions relating to each cornerstone.

---

1. Does your organization believe (at all levels and across all sectors and functions) that growth is central to value creation?

2. Have you articulated a growth vision that is highly visible and embedded?

3. Have you established a strong link between growth performance measures and rewards and recognition?

Exhibit 6.2. Cornerstone Diagnostic 1: Essential Practices for Commitment.

Testing for Commitment

Exhibit 6.2 gives the basic questions to answer about your organization's *commitment* cornerstone. An effective diagnostic for this cornerstone would be to use broad-based surveys followed by targeted interviews to test major conclusions and to probe for understanding.

For example, Practice 1 ("Believe deeply that growth drives value creation") can be addressed by survey questions such as this:

> Rank each of the following in order of priority to you in your job, using a scale of 1 to 10, with 10 being high.
>
> - Quality
> - Customer satisfaction
> - Profitability
> - Revenue growth
> - Employee satisfaction
> - Cost
> - Shareholder value

We typically incorporate these questions as part of a broader survey instrument, such as the Foundation Benchmarking Survey described later in this chapter.

Collecting information around Practice 2 ("Articulate a growth vision; embed it throughout the organization") requires more than simply being able to locate a document entitled "Growth Vision." The critical test is whether or not the vision is promoted and accepted broadly. For example, at Corning's corporate headquarters and at facilities around the globe hangs a blue banner with white lettering that says, "Growing Corning." In the lobby at headquarters and in all other principal building lobbies are displays showing how R&D, or marketing, or a particular product contributes to this goal. Check your own company's commitment to the practice by asking yourself, "Do we use any/many/enough pervasive reminders of growth?" Check to see whether the culture is replete with growth descriptors, such as the "Task Force on Growth" or the "Global Growth Initiative." Does your company work the language of growth into its day-to-day activities?

It is not sufficient to use such statements internally. Read both externally oriented and internal documents to see whether growth is emphasized. If growth is going to happen, all employees must hear about it, accept it, and adopt the vision.

For Practice 3 ("Link growth performance to reward and recognition"), there is an obvious analytical test. Simply check compensation systems to determine what drives them. But also look beyond compensation to other reward and recognition programs. Surveys work well here also. A compensation and reward system could be designed to encourage growth, but if people do not understand that it does or how it incorporates growth-oriented performance, its efficacy is compromised. We probe this issue by asking survey respondents to rank a series of related factors on a scale from 1 to 10 in terms of "how it is now" (actual), then follow up by asking "how you would like it to be" (desired). See the following sample.

"How well does top management emphasize growth?"

The management team for this example seems to be focused reasonably well on growth. A score of 7.3 is typical for a moderate-growth company. But respondents recommend kicking efforts up to an even higher level (the desired level of commitment is about 30 percent higher).

We use the following questions in the format just presented to probe the issue.

1. Is growth *pursued* as an important goal?
2. Does *top management* emphasize growth?
3. Does the company demonstrate its commitment to *long-term* growth?
4. Is the *entire company* committed to growth?

These four questions probe whether growth is emphasized in action as well as words (question 1), whether everyone buys into growth (questions 2 and 4), and whether the commitment will be sustained (question 3). We then ask a critical fifth question:

5. Are you *rewarded* for increasing revenues?

The first four questions test the extent of commitment, whereas the last question checks whether rewards are linked to growth day-to-day. It probes not whether the systems are designed with growth in mind, but, more importantly, whether people on the firing line know it. It is a way of gauging whether a sharp growth bias drives their behavior, which is critical.

Figure 6.4 is a summary of the actual findings of this test of commitment with a midsized client company with roughly a dozen business units. The company was emerging from a period of portfolio restructuring and had begun to reorient its strategic priorities toward growth. The survey targeted the areas in which organizational commitment fell short. The results for Practice 1 show that senior leaders (with a score of 9 or more) clearly accept growth's role in value creation. But at the business unit level (with a score of 4), the message is not yet in place. The scores on Practice 2 highlight the lack of a visible and/or embedded vision. Finally, results for Practice 3 depict a modest senior-level growth-reward link and a minimal business unit connection between growth and rewards.

Growth System Practices	Potential Strengths/ Issues for Client
1. Believe deeply that growth drives value creation.	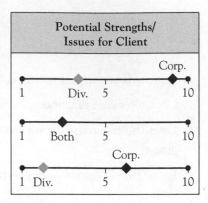
2. Articulate a growth vision and embed it throughout	
3. Link growth performance to rewards/recognition.	

Figure 6.4. Sample Diagnostic for Commitment.

Obviously, the starting point is for the company to diagnose the problem. This company now understands where it is out of alignment and by how much. In this company's case, only a few people have paid attention to the importance of growth. The starting point must be building a solid and deeply embraced commitment to growth. Next, the leaders must create a link between performance and rewards to embed the vision in their organization.

Testing for Strategy

The diagnosis and analysis of an organization's strategy cornerstone follow the same logic and process as for an evaluation of commitment. Check whether your organization is using the essential practices associated with strategy. Benchmarks work especially well for this diagnostic. For instance, for Practice 4 ("Create a Valuable Formula as a platform for long-term growth"), use the examples from Chapter Four as benchmarks. Does your company have as cleanly defined a focus as Boston Beer Company does? Can you fill in a Valuable Formula model as completely for your major products as Sprint can for SprintSense? Are all elements of the Valuable Formula coherent and do they reinforce one another? Check Exhibit 6.3 for a way to start diagnosing your organization's growth strategy.

A helpful way to check your progress on Practice 4 ("Create a Valuable Formula as a platform for long-term growth") is to divide

4. Have you created and specified clearly a Valuable Formula as a platform for long-term growth?

5. Do you manage the Valuable Formula across the growth cycle?

6. When you globalize your Valuable Formula, do you maintain its integrity while making it relevant locally?

7. Do you leverage the two key strategic weapons—innovation and alliances—to exploit Valuable Formulas?

Exhibit 6.3. Cornerstone Diagnostic 2: Essential Practices for Strategy.

your diagnostic team into two separate groups. Have one team articulate your Valuable Formula. Working independently, charter a second team to describe the Valuable Formula for your most troublesome competitor. When the two teams come together to compare results, you will have a crisper picture of your own formula burnished by the contrast.

To gain perspective on your competence around Practice 5 ("Manage the Valuable Formula across the growth cycle"), check different aspects of the process separately:

- Find recent examples of the creation of new products or services. Compare the number of potential new products in the pipeline to the number two years ago. Can you identify people or teams especially adept at the *create* phase? What are they doing now?

- Estimate the percentage of revenue generated by products in the *exploit* phase. How has it changed in the past two to three years?

- Identify when or if you successfully navigated a major *transition*. How will you know when the next one is coming?

External benchmarks exist for Practice 5 as well. For example, companies that excel tend to have aggressive new product development goals that help force the cycle. As we noted in Chapter Four, HP targets a rapid growth cycle through its "60 in 2" goal; so does 3M with its reset "30 in 4" goal. Determine whether your company has set analogous targets and communicated them across the organization.

To diagnose your company's use of Practice 6 ("Globalize the Valuable Formula; maintain integrity and modify locally"), think of the *Men's Health* and Starbucks examples. Without question the starting point is a well-defined Valuable Formula. It must maintain integrity, but not be "frozen" in its initial incarnation, and must be sensitive to local custom, yet not so much so that it becomes virtually unrecognizable from one locale to another. We find that clients err equally on both ends of the spectrum. By first articulating the formula, then benchmarking against the success paradigms, your company can minimize the probability of either error.

An analysis of Practice 7 ("Leverage two key strategic weapons—innovation and alliances—to exploit Valuable Formulas") is the final diagnostic for the strategy cornerstone. Each of the strategic weapons (innovation and alliances) must be analyzed separately in terms of process. Look at how each activity is incorporated into the development of strategic initiatives that exploit the Valuable Formula. Check how your organization builds adjustments of its Valuable Formula into a rollout program. What is the role of innovation processes once a product is launched? How do R&D and marketing engage in an ongoing dialogue? When a new Valuable Formula is being launched, how often does the company look for strategic partners to help? Is a set of questions designed into the strategic plan asking for partners? Do you have a roster of potential partners to call on?

Corning's frequent use of alliances to move new technologies from the create to the exploit phase exemplifies the use of Practice 7. The Citibank-Travelers merger represents the epitome of an innovative alliance. Each intends to leverage its own product power and innovation with the other's distribution system. At least in strategic concept, the Citigroup merger represents a masterful use of an alliance structure to leverage separate, innovative Valuable Formulas.

As a summary, Figure 6.5 lists the practices in turn, along with a sample benchmark organization. Many clients we've worked with prefer to develop their own benchmarks, choosing companies in a closely related business sector or a familiar peer group. Another option is a local, noncompetitive company with which your management team has strong personal relationships. The ability to dig inside another organization with which you choose to benchmark provides deeper understanding and a more relevant contrast to your own organization.

Testing for Capability

Exhibit 6.4 lists some sample questions for beginning to diagnose your organization's capability for growth. The starting point is to create a process map similar to Figure 5.2 in Chapter Five. Each attribute of leadership, architecture, culture, processes, and knowledge must be designated in terms of its relevance to growth for your organization, as Practice 8 states ("Identify and nurture all growth-supporting processes").

Growth System Practices	Benchmarks
4. Create Valuable Formula as platform for long-term growth.	SPRINT
5. Manage Valuable Formula across the growth cycle.	HP: "60-IN-2"
6. Globalize the Valuable Formula; maintain integrity and modify locally.	MEN'S HEALTH
7. Leverage two key strategic weapons: innovation and alliances.	CITIGROUP

Figure 6.5. Sample Diagnostic for Strategy.

8. Can you identify your growth-supporting processes? How do you nurture and care for them, especially during periods of cost reduction?

9. How do your growth foundations compare to the "best of the best"? Is your goal to beat them?

10. Have you designed initiatives to align your growth foundation? Are you implementing those initiatives?

Exhibit 6.4. Cornerstone Diagnostic 3: Essential Practices for Capability.

The next step in the capability diagnosis is to analyze your use of Practice 9 ("Benchmark foundations with the 'best of the best' and aim to beat them"). Figure 6.6 gives you a starting point with a list of the five foundations and benchmarks for each in the United States and globally. Alternatively, you can develop your own benchmark partners. For example, one of our clients, a midsized family-held company, finds other family-held companies more meaningful than a large, public corporation such as GE. The client has studied and interviewed Rodale Press and found relevant comparisons, even though Rodale's business focus is far afield from their own industry. Choose companies that you can relate to, but make sure they provide a challenge, a stretch for your own capability, and are not merely a "feel good" or comfortable comparison. In this case, Rodale sets an appropriately high standard, especially around leadership, culture, and the use of knowledge. For example, the culture comparison with Rodale would incorporate both *what* the key characteristics of its culture are (very open and team oriented, with a high degree of sharing), and *how* it sustains it (the ubiquity of the tree icon). Thus, both the "what" and the "how" inform the comparative analysis.

A sample diagnostic for Practice 10 ("Design and implement initiatives to align foundations") is shown in Figure 6.7, which displays a client's performance versus our best-in-class high-growth company

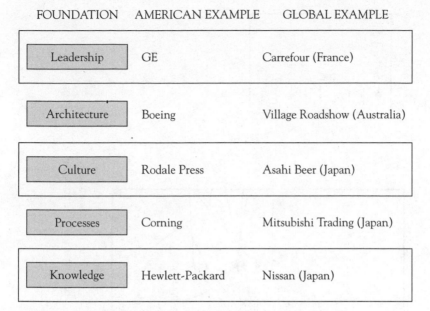

Figure 6.6. Potential Benchmarks for Each Foundation.

benchmark, represented by the shaded zone on the chart. Elements are tested across several foundations, focusing on innovation. In this case, the company is a manufacturer of technology-based products that has grown an average of 11 percent per year over five years. But its growth also has been erratic, going from as high as 25 percent to as low as 4 percent. The figure shows a company with a well-defined innovation process in place, but one that has lost its effectiveness. This was confirmed by an analysis of the company's new-product cycle time, which indicated that a key competitor could reach the market 15 to 20 percent faster.

Benchmark analyses such as this one are important "lead indicators" or early warning signs. The result desired is value-creating revenue growth. Revenue growth is a "lag" indicator, that is, it happens when the other indicators are in place. Figure 6.7 clearly shows the ineffectiveness of this company's current innovation process. It is a signal that the process is unlikely to deliver future

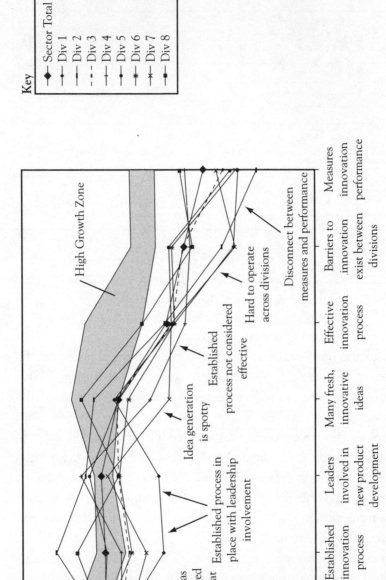

Key

| Sector Total |
| Div 1 |
| Div 2 |
| Div 3 |
| Div 4 |
| Div 5 |
| Div 6 |
| Div 7 |
| Div 8 |

High Growth Zone

Disconnect between measures and performance

Hard to operate across divisions

Established process not considered effective

Idea generation is spotty

Established process in place with leadership involvement

New ideas encouraged somewhat

10	Agree
9	
8	
7	
6	
5	"As Is" Scores
4	
3	
2	
1	
0	Disagree

Innovation encouraged

Established innovation process

Leaders involved in new product development

Many fresh, innovative ideas

Effective innovation process

Barriers to innovation exist between divisions

Measures innovation performance

Figure 6.7. Sample Diagnostic for Innovation Capability.

growth and, therefore, the process must be overhauled. The client currently is addressing the problem by comparing its innovation process practices with very large companies, such as Du Pont, to hone the ability to deal with the complexity of large scale, and with younger, smaller companies, such as NeoMagic, to recall important lessons central to entrepreneurs and other flexible, fast-growing organizations.

Figure 6.8 sums up the growth diagnostic for capability. We recommend not worrying too much about quantitative precision. Therefore, we tend to use a "stoplight" chart, which we will cover in more detail in Chapter Seven. It is fairly easy to summarize the status on each of the ten practices in the following way:

- Green indicates strong performance; equal to or better than "best of the best."

- Yellow represents middle-of-the-road performance, neither a cause for concern nor a strength to build on.

- Red flags a serious problem—an issue to be addressed immediately.

Growth System Practices	Benchmarks
8. Identify and nurture all growth-supporting processes.	**INDUSTRY PRINT**
9. Benchmark growth foundations with the "best-of-the-best" and aim to beat them.	**USE OURS; CREATE YOUR OWN**
10. Design and implement initiatives to align foundations.	**E. G., INNOVATION: DuPONT, NEOMAGIC**

Figure 6.8. Sample Diagnostic for Capability.

Conclusion

The description of the growth diagnostic test we have just described shows a primary advantage of diagnosing an organization's growth program. Namely, test results, because they are based on fact and are analytically rigorous, create a compelling case for change. Thus, the team develops buy-in early on and can quickly move to the next stage: Decide what to do to improve and take action steps to do so.

The three tests of the cornerstones of growth should help you define whether or not your company is aligned with the Growth System model of successful growth companies. You must stop to analyze your enterprise from the inside out. Our model provides the structure for such an analysis. Benchmarking against leading performers in each essential practice is a realistic challenge. By measuring against the best, your company can reset its own performance target. The Growth System is comprehensive and based on three cornerstones and ten essential practices. It works. Our basic tenets from the Introduction bear repeating at this point:

- Growth companies create value everywhere that matters.

- They do so through an intense, near-fanatical focus on growth.

- They align their entire enterprise to drive growth.

The Growth Challenge
Transformation to Growth Initiatives

If you diagnose properly, you no doubt will learn a great deal about your business practices and about how they are aligned for growth. Next you must address the issues that come up. What you learn is pointless if not applied to enhancing your organization's growth. With the diagnostic analysis in hand, the next steps are:

- To prioritize issues by estimating the magnitude of the gaps and the time and effort required to close them

- To resolve the issues in order to move toward full alignment with the growth system

Making the Case for Change

For most companies, a significant degree of change will be required to achieve the necessary alignment. The aftermath of the diagnostic may test your associates' commitment to growth. Because it is essential for them to commit fully to growth, the first step is to make sure everyone in the organization understands and accepts the need for change. Once they do, change becomes a necessary challenge, not a reason to retreat or stop altogether. Therefore, the first thing you must do is make a case for and build the business rationale for change.

At least four broad strategies are available for accomplishing this goal:

1. By fiat, by which a forceful leadership team, usually a new leadership team, announces the need to change in simple terms, such as "my way or the highway."

2. By empowerment, involving large numbers of people in the development process. At Becton-Dickinson, the leading manufacturer of medical devices and diagnostics, they accomplished this through a series of "town meetings," bringing thousands of employees on board early.[1] Presently, B-D is in the early stages of transforming itself back into the growth company it was once. By enacting a two-year program to involve everyone in the effort, the company has embedded the case for change deeply throughout the company.

3. By crisis, because an organization that believes it is in crisis pays attention and is motivated to find solutions. (One of our clients has triggered every major change in his organization over the past fifteen years in this way.)

4. By fact, that is, to build a compelling case for change because data and logic dictate it.

In practice, most leaders we know blend these strategies into their own personal approaches. The critical point is to develop a compelling, well-designed case for change. Do not underestimate the importance of this process. This finding was underscored recently at our fourth annual Growth Conference through a survey of the conference attendees,[2] comprised of senior executives from a broad range of companies. We asked them to estimate the relative importance of various factors in sustaining future growth. They rated "believing in the importance of growth" as the most critical factor for success, even over "the momentum created by a hot product." Our work with clients also confirms this fact. Thus, the first step in alignment is to ensure that your organization accepts growth as the goal.

Viewing the Battlefield

Recognizing the importance of the value-growth matrix, we know that if returns are poor (less than the cost of capital), growth will not create value. However, while restructuring to improve returns and become growth-ready, it is both possible and advisable to begin preparing for the growth journey. Clearly, it is crucial to take care of growth-supporting processes. For example, when restructuring, set different cost-reduction targets for those processes required to fuel future growth. Virtually all of the restructuring tasks should be shaped by the vision of future growth. Further, while you make the business case to validate restructuring, also build the core analytics to bracket the potential upside of future growth. Because growth is the superior value-creating strategy, give credit for it within the business case.

The results of the three tests of alignment you have done will provide direction for ensuing initiatives. It is rare that all of the tests would indicate equal shortcomings. Undoubtedly, some elements will be farther from the desired goal and be most critical to address first.

An Example of a Diagnostic

Figure 7.1 is an example of a diagnostic done for a client of ours that was determined to grow and dedicated to building a sustainable growth company. The figure illustrates how to know how to proceed after you have finished your own diagnosis. The scorecard in the figure is a high-level summary from the growth diagnostic team, set up like a stoplight, as we described in Chapter Six. Each of the summary points is backed up by additional detail and supporting analysis, of course.

Senior management first addressed the growth issue several years ago. The company operates globally, but was founded in the United States. Its revenues exceed $5 billion, and its growth rate is now in double digits, up from about 3 percent per year in the period from

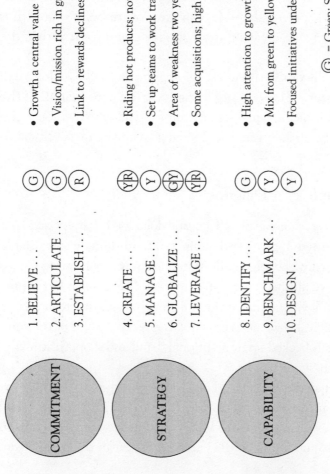

COMMITMENT

1. BELIEVE . . . . ⓖ • Growth a central value
2. ARTICULATE . . . ⓖ • Vision/mission rich in growth imagery
3. ESTABLISH . . . . Ⓡ • Link to rewards declines beyond top 10%

STRATEGY

4. CREATE . . . . Ⓨ|Ⓡ • Riding hot products; not clear on their "essence"
5. MANAGE . . . Ⓨ • Set up teams to work transition
6. GLOBALIZE . . . Ⓖ|Y • Area of weakness two years ago; high priority to resolve
7. LEVERAGE . . . . Ⓨ|Ⓡ • Some acquisitions; high degree of insular behavior

CAPABILITY

8. IDENTIFY . . . . ⓖ • High attention to growth processes
9. BENCHMARK . . . Ⓨ • Mix from green to yellow to red
10. DESIGN . . . . Ⓨ • Focused initiatives underway

ⓖ = Green: Strong alignment; possible area of strength
Ⓨ = Yellow: Moderate alignment; not immediate concern
Ⓡ = Red: Misaligned; primary problem

Figure 7.1. Scorecard Summary.

1990 to 1993. The company sells both products and related services and is shifting toward increasing the services portion. The company's cash flow return on investment exceeds its cost of capital by several points. Thus, its growth focus and accelerating momentum are appropriate.

In this case, the decision to grow had already been made. We can infer from the scorecard that the case for growth had been made to the company at large because two of the three commitment practices scored green. Also, some of the shortcomings to success had been identified and initiatives undertaken to resolve them. For example, the company was U.S.-dominated, with 75 percent of revenues generated domestically in 1990. It has begun to move aggressively to achieve greater balance. The organization is implementing its goal to grow revenues outside the Americas twice as fast as it grows domestic sales.

The only red light in the commitment section, a gap between growth rhetoric and growth rewards, was both obvious and typical. Clearly, the problem was the compensation system. Only the most senior management, less than the top 10 percent of all employees, had a direct link between growth and rewards. Other levels of management had base compensation set by dollars of assets or revenues that they managed. Some would say this inspires managers to grow, to increase their scope, thus setting a new, larger base compensation (a trickle-down reward policy). However, to field managers and associates the link seemed remote. Further, organizational memory of defeat lasts a long time. The risk of failure kept people back. The red light was an accurate description of a problem. Although any red light naturally needs attention, compensation systems are especially visible. Changes to reward systems send a strong signal. Our client now plans to roll out a revised compensation system strongly emphasizing growth.

The leaders of this organization also addressed the fear of failure we mentioned. They realized that companies that grow make mistakes, but they recover, learn, and move on. This company has decided as part of its charter to teams taking on significant growth challenges to give a specific safety net, a guarantee to fall back on, if the growth initiative comes up short. Their safety net is becoming a "best practice" process. In broad terms, it creates a peer group for the growth team, allowing an unsuccessful growth team to reenter the ongoing line organization at the same compensation level as the peer group has achieved at that point. If the growth initiative works, the team members become heroes, with the attendant rewards. At worst, they lose no ground to their peers. Needless to say, very talented people are volunteering to take on growth initiatives in this organization.

Let's look at the strategy cornerstone in Figure 7.1. It requires attention. This client has created Valuable Formulas. In fact, several of its products currently are very hot. The company has been highly opportunistic—quick to identify a new trend and respond to it. Perhaps "fast follower" is the most apt description of its strategic bent. However, when pressed to articulate the essence of its Valuable Formula on the model, the company falls short. In being responsive and following quickly, it is guessing at the most important product features and customer needs. Management intends to set up two independent teams to model their product versus the product of the earlier-to-market competitor to deal with this issue. Chartering these teams, which have senior management involvement and broad visibility, signals their seriousness about growth, a positive sign to the rest of the company even before results are evident.

Not all solutions to their problems are so straightforward. Addressing the yellow/red score of Practice 7 will take longer. The underlying analytics depict a company willing to pursue acquisitions but uncomfortable with other forms of alliances. Acquiring businesses to gain access to new markets makes sense to the company management only when they can fully integrate the new company. They are not flexible on this issue. We term this "insular behavior," and it can compromise future growth. It is an observable fact that growth companies form a large number of alliances and that these alliances span a variety of types, including but not limited to wholly owned acquisitions. To break out of their insularity, this company must first accept that its practice of fully integrating every new acquisition is a problem. Then, it can move to modify its behavior throughout the organization. At this point, the issue has been identified but is not being dealt with.

The results for the capability cornerstone in Figure 7.1 show excellent scores on some of the essential practices. The green light symbolizes a high degree of attention to growth-supporting processes. However, the yellow light for benchmarking requires a closer look. Figure 7.2 is a more detailed analysis of the foundations that make up the capability cornerstone. Clearly, the red score for architecture must be addressed.

As a matter of fact, architecture has been flagged red for more than a year. The client accepts the designation, but making a change is a matter of priority and degree of difficulty. To truly attack the problem of organizational architecture would require a

GROWTH FOUNDATION	SCORE
LEADERSHIP	GREEN — Excellent leadership development programs. Active mentoring and counseling.
ARCHITECTURE	RED — Matrix-style organization "tired" at best. Too many one-off decisions to deal with complexity.
CULTURE	GREEN — Continuing emphasis yielding measurable results.
PROCESS	GREEN/YELLOW — Revamped innovation process. Alliances need work.
KNOWLEDGE	YELLOW — Hardest to do well. Not at a disadvantage versus competition nor a decided strong suit.

Figure 7.2. A Closer Look at the Foundations of Capability.

complicated and innovative redesign. In this case, we have drawn a critical yet subtle distinction. We have not allowed the client to shirk an important challenge. This client's leaders are informed and concerned. However, they know that a competitor recently implemented a bold new organizational design that has been spectacularly unsuccessful. This client's leadership team does not shy away from challenge. On the leadership foundation, it has implemented new leadership development programs that were once considered too comprehensive, time-consuming, and costly. Today, these programs are seen as the best such programs in their industry and arguably close to GE's world-class level. However, architecture, especially in terms of organizational design, is in a "watch and study" category, not yet a focus for a bold initiative. They are not ignoring the problem. Rather, they are dealing with it using short-term solutions while still seeking an innovative, grand design. To pretend that it did not exist would be foolish, but to keep the issue out front and manage it while searching for a solution is a very reasonable tactic of an informed and capable leadership team. Sometimes this approach is best.

We have included this example to show where your organization should be headed. Your goal should be to create a similar picture of your company with each essential practice and each foundation scored as green, yellow, or red. Armed with this information, your organization can design and then implement corrective initiatives—or choose to watch and study.

Tackling the Issues

Figure 7.3 depicts a matrix of the key issues any company must diagnose before deciding which are critical and how to deal with them. This is the ultimate goal, where analysis becomes galvanized into practice. In Figure 7.3, we have identified the four key issues that our client must deal with and the type of initiative that is required to resolve each.

The initiative categories are straightforward, namely:

Issue	Initiative Category					
	Communication	Training	Process	Structure	Strategy	Metrics
COMMITMENT Reward/Performance Link	*		**			**
STRATEGY Valuable Formula Defined		*			**	*
STRATEGY Insular re Alliances	**	**	**			*
CAPABILITY Architecture "Tired"	*	*	*	**		*

Figure 7.3. Matrix of Key Issues and Required Initiatives.
** = most important; * = supporting.

- Communication: "Tell them what you mean."

- Training: "Teach them how to do it."

- Process: "Design or redesign to do it better."

- Structure: "Reorganize the teams and tasks."

- Strategy: "Rework your Valuable Formulas and/or how to play them out."

- Metrics: "Set targets; measure progress."

For the commitment issue (weakness in the reward-performance link), explaining how the reward system works requires some communication. However, of greater importance is the process of redesigning the reward systems themselves. Embedding metrics to measure progress completes the resolution of the issue. For the first strategy issue, building a coherent and articulate Valuable Formula takes precedence. Once that has been done successfully, training programs can be utilized to share the competency more widely. Again, metrics must be in place to gauge progress and to monitor change. The second strategy issue, insular behavior, is a big leadership challenge requiring communication, training, and a process. All three may be equally influential. Metrics can be used to measure progress. The capability issue, revamping tired architecture, will require a major structural redesign. In the short term, minor process modifications, some training and monitoring, and plenty of communication must suffice.

By using such a matrix to show the problems that have been identified and the initiatives required for their solution, you and your company will be prepared to move toward resolution. In fact, the client we are using as an example has not waited. The compensation problem has been tackled and virtually fixed. Initiatives have been designed, and teams have been chartered to tackle the other problems. Given their focus on growth and the effort they are putting into achieving alignment, we think they will make it. We bet they will sail into the millennium with a Growth System embedded in the fabric of the company's culture and processes, actions and strategies. And we bet they will continue to outperform their more slow-growing counterparts, everywhere that matters.

This sample of how to use the growth diagnostic was, we hope, helpful to you on your own journey to value-creating growth. Your own diagnostic should follow a similar process. There are no typical results. Your diagnostic will be different from any other. The diagnostic is simultaneously structured and creative. Is "structured creativity" an oxymoron? Certainly not. A well-formed process frees up creative thoughts and actions. After all, the best innovation processes have well-designed formal approaches and metrics. Creativity thrives. Take the growth diagnostic seriously. Work on its directives and, like our client, outperform your more slow-growing competitors, everywhere that matters.

Part III

Aligning the Enterprise

Beginning the Journey

On our journey to discover and inculcate the secrets of value-creating growth, the summit is within reach. Having covered the basic principles and dealt with specific growth issues, we can understand that the Growth System is founded on three solid structures—commitment, strategy, and capability. Of course, we recognize that new issues always come up. A successful company will never be short of issues to confront. A recognition of this fact is built into the Growth System at the most fundamental level. We must forever manage the growth cycle. Continual evaluation and re-creation are inherent to our success. We will draw on the familiar patterns and practices of the growth system as we've described it to tackle whatever comes.

In this third part of the book, we focus on how a company acts when growth is so central that management of the whole company is structured around the need for growth and a system to drive it. We will focus on three clients as examples. Each demonstrates how to make growth the process that governs everything from day-to-day activities to long-term business strategies. We will focus on three aspects of growth:

1. *Setting Up a Growth Agenda.* We will discuss how you can set up a growth agenda for your company so that growth is the focus of all management team discussions, new tactics, and future maneuvering.

2. *Designing Growth into Key Processes.* We will describe how the growth cycle can be utilized to restructure the strategic planning process or any other organizational processes.

3. *Testing Periodically to Stay Aligned with Growth Goals.* We show how to do a diagnostic analysis to ensure that your company remains aligned with your growth goals. The saying, "What goes around, comes around," for our purposes here, means what you emphasize and repeat will come back to you.

This part of the book, then, gives a vision of victory in your organization's growth journey, when growth becomes the process that governs everything from day-to-day duties to long-term business strategies.

8

When Growth Becomes the Process
What Growth Looks Like

Our hope is that you will use this book as an instructional guide-book, akin to a do-it-yourself manual. If so, you will eventually lay the closed book on a desk, depart from the warm light of your study and enter the harsh fluorescence of your office. This brings us to a crucial point: Theories are impotent without implementation. Consider the Growth System to be a hammer. You are the carpenter, and your company and its employees are raw materials. Take what you have learned here as though you had a case of tools to assist you in constructing your company in a way that meets your growth goals.

In our quest to indoctrinate you about the importance of growth, we have used an array of concepts to breathe life into key ideas. It has been our goal both to create a vision and to outline the journey you must undertake to grasp that vision. You must build, fire up, and drive a growth engine. We will describe the journeys of three other companies that have traveled the road before you and help you to see how they have achieved success or faltered along the way.

Example: Setting Up a Growth Agenda

One of our growth clients came to us after a ten-year history of growth had suddenly faltered. After a decade of revenue increases, the company's growth had become very erratic. The company CEO concluded that he had to stabilize growth at higher, sustainable levels. He also realized something very important at the outset, namely that he and his company had to define what success would look like. This would give them not only a goal to strive for, but a structure to follow to reach that goal.

The CEO was very candid and specific, saying, "We have found nearly forty issues in which we are deficient. If you come up with numbers forty-one, forty-two, and forty-three, I'm going to be upset." He understood a key operating principle: to prioritize deficiencies. He was already in "issue overload" and did not need more. He wanted us to tell him which were the most important obstacles to his organization's growth—those primary challenges that had caused the company to stumble. He wanted to solve the most important challenges first.

After cataloging the issues (amazingly, we did find forty), we set about prioritizing which were most threatening to his company's growth goals. For example, lack of a clear message articulating the importance of growth had left the organization unfocused. We also found that inconsistent new product flow was less about a lack of fresh ideas and more about an underpowered and overly complex process to capture and nurture new product candidates. Like the CEO, we had our own priorities. Remember the takeaway from Chapter Six: "When your company is not growing, your first priority is to jump-start your growth engine *now*." Besides trying to meet the CEO's needs, we looked for those issues that, if remedied, would promote short-term results. For example, refurbishing an already existing but tired Valuable Formula could yield fairly immediate, tangible outcomes. In contrast, creating a brand-new formula for a new market might yield more long-run value, but might require a year or more before tangible results would be evident.

In addition, we separated each of the priorities into major and minor actions required, then estimated the degree of difficulty to complete each. Besides knowing the expected payoff of each, we knew how long each task would take and how much effort would be required. Our objective was to give the CEO a clear vision of where to direct his team's energies.

Figure 8.1 shows the hierarchy of growth initiatives we created. We organized around four critical priorities: high-performance market-driven innovation, enhanced product management competence, sophisticated understanding of business economics and value, and clear strategic intent. Starting from the left, market-driven innovation leads to excellence in the create phase and enhanced product management leads to excellence in the exploit phase, and so on. The objective of our effort, as we have said, was to set up a framework to direct management attention, with a sharp focus on growth. By dealing with each priority, our client would be able to improve the ability to sustain growth within and across the full cycle. At present, the CEO uses a somewhat more complex graphic than the one in Figure 8.1 to organize the agenda for monthly management meetings, as well as to broaden planning efforts.

To accomplish any major turnaround, first ask yourself, "What does my growth agenda look like?" Now that we have analyzed many companies according to our diagnostic, we have found in most cases that a company is paying close attention to costs and not much attention to growth. For example, another client of ours once mused over the fact that she didn't think the strategic business unit (SBU) heads in her organization were sufficiently worried about growth. She felt they were not implementing enough initiatives to promote growth. She pointed to their recent mediocre growth rate (4 percent per year) as hard evidence. We asked to see the minutes from their most recent monthly management meeting. What we found was not surprising. The minutes demonstrated a lack of attention to growth by senior management, not by the SBU heads. The CEO had directed the managers to spend the first three hours of the four-hour meeting on "line 30," or the item in their budget that communicated variance from planned earnings in the past month. Then, they spent another half-hour on assorted issues of the month, only devoting the final half-hour (just an eighth of their time) to

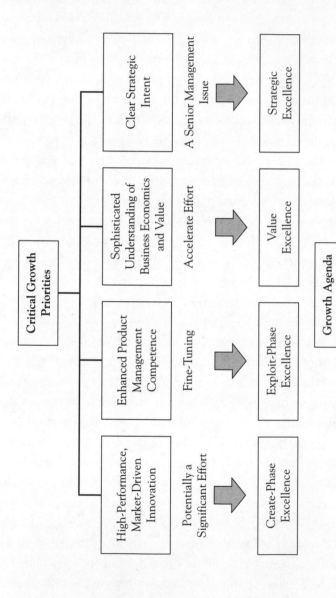

Figure 8.1. Sample of a Chart to Help a Client Focus on the Growth Agenda.

growth. Placing such a weighty emphasis on variations from planned monthly earning was far too much short-term thinking. We pointed out that if the allotments were reversed, giving growth three-quarters of the attention, the SBUs would naturally focus more closely and more often on growth and the future of the company. That advice was given four years ago. That client's business in now clicking along at 25 percent growth per year. This example demonstrates how easy it is to become dominated by the day-to-day dilemmas. If you do not take the time to look to the future, the daily routine will overwhelm you. The solution is to stick to your growth agenda, which helps you see the horizon. Of course, you should not ignore the short-term issues. Just strike a better long-term/short-term balance. Reverse the order of your management topics occasionally, especially when you notice that less time and effort are being spent on future growth.

Designing Growth into Key Processes

When we described the growth cycle in Chapter Four, we introduced it as an operating practice, not a motivational theory. The cycle guides and defines management. This sentiment was echoed by George Bodway of Hewlett-Packard in his presentation given to our third annual Growth Conference in June 1997.[1] His speech provided an example of how Growth System elements influence Hewlett-Packard's management processes. In our terminology, businesses are characterized by their evolutionary state: create, exploit, transition. Hewlett-Packard's SBU managers know that, in the exploit phase, the point is about driving your business to maximum revenue and cash flow via a well-structured Valuable Formula. Such business units are in the "execute, don't add!" phase. In short, businesses in the exploit phase will receive the lion's share of capital allocated to them, as they are seeking to optimize value creation while the formula is hot. Literally, HP's strategic financial and tactical decisions are implemented according to the cycle. Figure 8.2 represents visually how HP has organized its strategic planning process to be consistent with the growth cycle. The growth cycle is not a trite metaphor spoken about at meetings, nor merely a way to conceptualize an organization. It is actions and practices.

There must be a constant awareness of all three phases of the cycle. The cycle, by design, challenges business leaders to compete with their own ideas and Valuable Formulas. The successful company poses questions such as "How long will our current products last?" and "What are we doing to refresh or re-create our formula when and if a transition occurs?" Keep the cycle in mind as a symbol of the cliché that the only constant is change. The message for businesses to remember in their *create* phases is the constant need to take ideas from the formative stage into the competitive marketplace—to *exploit* their ideas. Of course, the *transition* phase, when the value of an idea has been exhausted, is the time to re-create the formula or trash old for new.

Strategic Business Planning Processes, Tools, and Their Positioning
Managers of Multiple Businesses

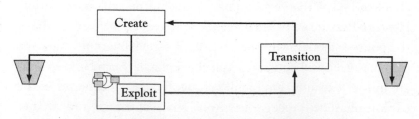

Figure 8.2. HP Organization According to the Growth Cycle.

Any important process can and should be designed around growth. In HP's case the growth cycle framework serves as a structure for its strategy and resource allocation debates. In your company you could apply similar logic, asking questions such as the following at the SBU level:

- *Create-Phase SBUs.* Are you funding enough R&D? Because results (the ultimate measures of success) come later, how are you measuring interim progress? How will you cross the create-exploit chasm?

- *Exploit-Phase SBUs.* Are value metrics in place at virtually all levels? What early warning signals do you have to anticipate major changes to your current Valuable Formula?

- *Transition-Phase SBUs.* How will you decide when to give up versus reinvent? How will you maintain morale when growth is not happening, especially if most other SBUs are growing?

Testing Periodically to Stay Aligned with Growth Goals

Basically, to twist an aphorism, we want to train old dogs to do old tricks. Don't be afraid to chase your own tail, to attempt to catch up to and surpass yourself. There is value in a focused, if not full, reapplication of the growth diagnostic. The necessity for continual self-analysis is what we term the "diagnostic revolution" (seen in Figure 8.3). If your original diagnostic (Phase 0) uncovers a shortcoming or misalignment, your company must prioritize the issues, then create initiatives to fill the gaps and ensure alignment (Phase 1). That leads you back to your basics, at which time the fundamental principles must be relearned and honed, then the issues tackled again and alignment tested again (Phase 2).

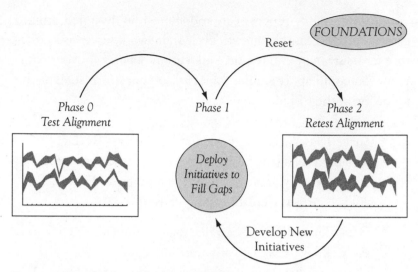

Figure 8.3. The Diagnostic Revolution.

At this stage, having understood what growth takes and implemented actions to achieve it, your organization is clearly striving to make growth the process. Eventually, whether you pass or fail any one diagnostic, you will always want to do analysis. The process is twofold: (1) check to see whether basic initiatives have worked, and (2) diagnose again to uncover any new problems.

A third client serves as an example of this construct. We helped build the basics for this particular client in 1993–1994. The company was a major player in an industry that was growing at 8 to 10 percent per year. But this company was growing only at 5 to 6 percent, thus losing market share. We began by assisting the client to realign itself with the growth-success model, our Growth System. As the basics began to be covered, we were able to isolate and assist the company to pursue key issues, such as extending their global reach. At present, they are growing at 12 to 15 percent per year with new businesses being created and some existing major businesses soaring over 30 percent!

This client has the potential to keep on growing. Yet, we just completed a second growth diagnostic to update it and to ensure that initiatives are working and that the company remains aligned for growth. Our first diagnostic in 1993 isolated numerous growth-sapping limitations. We used it to reset the new management agenda on growth. The 1998 diagnostics are especially focused on the best performing businesses to anticipate any emerging slow-growth issues before they became significant problems. Figure 8.3 depicts how the diagnostic can be used continually to update progress.

The diagnostic may seem unnecessary in high-performance SBUs. One could think that a client's recent strong revenue growth, gain in market share, and record profits mean that all initiatives had taken hold. On the contrary, although the indicators showed a rapidly firing growth engine, our recent diagnostic of this client unveiled two critical factors that could threaten future growth. The first deficiency was in their general growth orientation regarding a key foundation (processes), specifically a lack of competency in forming alliances. During globalization and expansion, business took them to countries where they had no experience and no real contacts. Instead of making wise alliances with outside parties, who could fill the cultural gaps they were encountering, the client had tried to do everything itself. The company was much too insular. It must now learn how to build and manage constructive alliances. The second deficiency we uncovered was that the company's growth was based in large measure on the huge success of one very profitable Valuable Formula. This formula drives present growth, but no formula can promise never-ending results. This issue had an obvious solution. The client has formed a high-profile team to research customer needs in order to create a new Valuable Formula before the current one fades.

A caveat is worth raising here. Repeating the growth diagnostic has enormous value when it casts light on a previously undiscovered growth issue. However, the original diagnostic and all repetitions come with a price. Namely, by spotlighting a specific growth issue, the diagnostic creates high expectations for change throughout the organization. If appropriate growth initiatives are not implemented, the organization often loses confidence in its leaders. A repeat diagnostic in such a case would portray a devastating scene: a lack of progress or failure. Always remember that the growth diagnostic is such a powerful tool.

Takeaway

The growth diagnostic is a powerful tool: The expectation for meaningful, productive change must be met.

We counsel our clients to attack the growth issue aggressively. We also remind them that, once initiated, you must deliver. When the business case for growth is made and the organization accepts the daunting challenge for the glorious reward, you must deliver. With this risk in mind, it is again important to think about our takeaway: "When your company is not growing, your first priority is to jump-start your growth engine *now*." Execute immediately those efforts you think will take you on the shortest path to growth. Diagnose, then act quickly and aggressively.

Conclusion

We have presented just three examples from the many arenas that companies have focused on to make growth the core management process. All three examples featured real companies, operating in the real world, putting forth tremendous effort to achieve their goals. However, they illustrate universal principles. In that respect, the companies are exactly like your company, and your company can learn to be like them.

9

Epilogue

With all the research and methodology to support it, our asser-
tions about growth still leave one question unasked: Is
growth a fad? You should rightfully be cautious of the "fad du jour,"
as racks and racks are added to your local bookseller's business section and promptly filled with the newest, most contemporary
advice. However, even if we were to assume the reprehensible—
that growth is another management fad—it shines brightly as a
worthwhile one. Akin to the fitness or anti-smoking movements,
the evidence is overwhelming in its support. As demonstrated in
the Introduction, the link between growth and performance is very
strong. As we said, the results of twenty years of client service, cou-
pled with four years of dedicated, growth-centered research, indicate that high-growth companies realize five to ten times the returns
to shareholders as slow-growth companies. For customers, high-
growth companies churn out new products and services at nearly
twice the "normal" rate. In the last five years, a mere two hundred
companies (less than 2 percent of all public companies) created 32
percent of all jobs. Employees love working in high-growth organizations in spite of intense pressure to perform. Even if it is a fad,
growth delivers on its promise. On that basis alone, it has a future.

Growth also has a distinguished past. The term "long-range planning" gained currency at many consulting firms, such as Arthur D.
Little, in the late 1960s, and it marked the first move to incorporate

growth formally into the corporate mind-set. Bruce Henderson then formed the Boston Consulting Group in the 1970s around the concept of "strategy," adding useful analytics. Henderson's theory hinged on such insights as the growth-share matrix. He depicted it as a 2-by-2 display that charted market growth (a surrogate for a company's growth potential) versus market share (a surrogate for competitive position). The major proviso of the matrix was that if a company achieved a greater scale, that is, a greater market share than its competitors, it would be more profitable. This assertion was confirmed by such studies as those conducted by Robert Buzzell at the Harvard Business School[1] in the late 1970s. Of course, in order to become larger than a competitor, a company had to outgrow the competition. For this newly defined strategy, growth had to be the answer.

In keeping with this roughly thirty-year history as business strategists, we believe growth will continue to deliver results in the high-performance arena. If you want to be mediocre, you can accept low-growth targets; but if you seek high performance, the odds of success increase sharply, not marginally, when you grow fast. In the near future, we see a surge of growth success stories that will serve to bolster a widespread acceptance of sustainable growth strategies. If Jack Welch and General Electric do become the first $70 billion growth company, other heretofore moribund companies can and will be inspired to try. If Hewlett-Packard can avoid the dreaded growth stall that so many other companies have encountered, it will give others confidence that growth on a large scale, like the once-insurmountable four-minute mile, is a psychological barrier rather than a physical one. Recall that in the early 1950s, the implied consequences of running a mile in less than four minutes were that the lungs would explode, leg muscles would erupt from their fascia sheaths—the feat was considered an impossibility. Then, one day in May 1954, a young English medical student named Roger Bannister barely slipped under the mark by 0.6 second. Not only did he not die, but days later, an Australian, John Landry, knocked a few more tenths off the record, and more athletes followed soon thereafter. Growth at large scale is an analog. Once a company breaks through, many others will follow. If small companies take the time to reinforce their commitment to growth, to execute growth-capturing strategies, and to invest in their capability for the future, a whole new generation of large, successful value-creating growth companies will evolve. Each new story will be a step on which others may confidently tread.

In fairness, we admit that happy endings depend on confronting at least two "mega-issues." First, very large companies seeking long-term growth must conquer growth at scale and overcome the growth stall. The cases of GE and HP are real-life examples of this challenge. Mega-mergers in the pharmaceutical industry are also. Obviously, the longer a company grows, the bigger it becomes. So all growth companies essentially aspire to what now seems to be a threatening situation. The problem may seem insurmountable. A large company's greatest problem is its own size. Within huge corporations, it is hard to communicate ideas, hard to understand all directives and operational details, hard to empower people to perform when they seem like insignificant specks in a vast universe. All extremely large companies face this problem and recognize its importance. As they strive to overcome it and emerge successful, we will have more confidence in our own abilities to reach and surpass similar plateaus.

The second mega issue is managing growth across an increasingly broad, far-flung, and complex network of strategic alliances. This problem has two edges. On one hand, forming alliances is necessary for successful high-growth companies and can be a solution to the growth stall. Leveraging another organization's strengths can help to overcome the limitation of size. A network provides competencies that can be shared as opposed to being owned by one company. As we have learned, successful growth companies execute numerous alliances and learn to do so effectively.

On the other hand, managing growth across alliances requires communicating a coherent Growth System (commitment, strategy, and capability) across many partners in different parts of the globe. Although alliances are a necessary prerequisite for growth, the challenge comes from the increased complexity of operations. As the number of alliances grows arithmetically, the complexity grows geometrically, perhaps exponentially. As with the problems of scale, our growth champions must solve this issue as well.

As the growth pioneers must do, remember what you now know about growth. Growth delivers on the promise of superior performance. Growth creates value everywhere that matters. Although growth is hard, it is also a learned competence. These are research-based findings underscored by experience that should serve to inspire us all. Any obstacles to growth must not be seen as deterrents, but as the reasons to collaborate, investigate, and discover all of the secrets to growth in order to reap the rewards. Growth's promise of creating value everywhere that matters is why we have worked so hard at understanding and promoting it, and why we remain dedicated to teaching and pursuing value-creating growth as far into the future as we can see.

May the promise of growth guide you as well.

Why stay we on the Earth except to grow?

Robert Browning[2]

Appendix A

Notes on Methodology

When the Growth Team was chartered in the spring of 1994, under the leadership of coauthor Tom Doorley, it designed a research-based, experience-tested methodology. Professor James Brian Quinn of Dartmouth's Amos Tuck School of Business Administration advised us as we developed the research construct and methodology.

The basic Growth Team goals were as follows:

Research-Oriented Goals

- Identify patterns of success and failure in achieving and sustaining growth.

- Define strategies, actions, and capabilities that foster growth.

- Develop a conceptual framework for long-term success.

Client-Oriented Goals

- Develop new tools and methodologies to assist clients to achieve and sustain growth.

- Share learning with clients early and often.

These goals were modified in mid-1995 as our knowledge deepened. At that point, we decided to tighten the focus to efforts to create value through growth. Our major learnings at this point were (1) that performance is the overarching, ongoing goal, and (2) that growth is the superior strategy to achieve it.

To guide us we created a basic definition of growth as "revenue change over medium-term to long-term, that is, five, ten, or twenty years." We determined that any one year's growth is less important but that the trend was of central importance. Our primary interest was in growth driven by increased value, new products and services, and alliances. We concluded that growth did *not* mean continuous, top-line growth. In fact, we discovered that an apparently "stagnant" company (in total revenues) can effectively be managing some units that are growing.

Our basic data sources were as follows:

Secondary Research

- For comparability of financial data, we used Standard & Poor's Compustat data, which included approximately 30,000 companies, globally, over five-, ten-, and twenty-year periods.

Primary Research

- We created a proprietary database of "growth partners," a group of seventy-five companies (see Exhibit I.1 in the Introduction for a representative list) that our Growth Team analyzed in depth.

- We used proprietary, broad-based surveys, such as Braxton Associates' Growth Foundation Benchmarking Survey.

- We used internal client information and experience from our case files.

Fundamental to our learning processes was a technique we called "contrasts of the extremes," that is, comparing the extremes, such as high-growth/high-performance companies versus low-growth/low-performance companies. After dramatic contrasts and broad themes were established, we considered companies between the extremes to round out our understanding of how to apply our major findings.

Finally, we worked hard to test our evolving findings in the "real world." For example, we shared our insights with clients regularly. Further, we spoke in numerous venues, often on the same program with those with other points of view. The Conference Board has been an especially valuable ally, providing six senior management seminar opportunities. We refined our message significantly based on these interactions.

Appendix B

Growth-Related Source Material

During the course of our work, we have uncovered many valuable sources of insight. Here is a selection of sources that could provide additional perspective.

Historical Foundations

Drucker, P. *Concept of the Corporation*. New York: Day, 1972.
McGregor, D. *The Human Side of Enterprise*. (25th anniversary ed.) New York: McGraw-Hill, 1985.
Ogilvy, D. *Ogilvy on Advertising*. New York: Crown, 1983.
Penrose, E. *The Theory of the Growth of the Firm*. (8th ed.) Oxford: Oxford University Press, 1995.

Commitment

Collins, J., and Porras, J. *Built to Last*. New York: HarperCollins, 1994.

Strategy

Gordon, W.J.J. *Synectics*. New York: HarperCollins, 1961.
Henderson, B. *Henderson on Corporate Strategy*. Cambridge, Mass.: Abt, 1979.
Solman, P., and Friedman, T. *Life and Death on the Corporate Battlefield*. New York: Simon & Schuster, 1982.

Capability

Peters, T., and Waterman, R. *In Search of Excellence*. New York: HarperCollins, 1982.

Architecture

Quinn, J. B. *The Intelligent Enterprise*. New York: Free Press, 1992.

Leadership

Kouzes, J., and Posner, B. *The Leadership Challenge: How to Get Extraordinary Things Done in Organizations*. San Francisco: Jossey-Bass, 1990.

Culture

Bennis, W. *Organizing Genius*. Reading, Mass.: Addison-Wesley, 1997.

Deal, T., and Kennedy, A. *Corporate Cultures*. Reading, Mass.: Addison-Wesley, 1982.

Processes

Hammer, M. *Beyond Reengineering: How the Process-Centered Organization Is Reshaping Our Work and Our Lives*. New York: HarperBusiness, 1996.

Knowledge

Davis, S., and Botkin, J. *The Monster Under the Bed: How Business Is Mastering the Opportunity of Knowledge for Profit*. New York: Simon & Schuster, 1995.

Negroponte, N. *Being Digital*. New York: Knopf, 1995.

Nonaka, I., and Takeuchi, H. *Knowledge-Creating Companies*. Oxford: Oxford University Press, 1995.

Growth-Related Articles

Avila, J., Moss, N., and Furchan, M. "Keys to Profitable Growth." *McKinsey Quarterly*, 1996, *1*, 202.

Cook, J., and McGrath, M. "Growing in the Food Industry." *McKinsey Quarterly*, 1996, *1*, 198–201.

Darwent, C., and Knobel, L. "Faster and Faster Growth." *WorldLink*, Mar.-Apr. 1997, 47–53.

Doorley, T. "Real Growth/Real Value." *WorldLink*, Mar.-Apr. 1996, 44–45.

Doorley, T. "Global Foundations for Global Growth." *WorldLink*, Mar.-Apr. 1997, 44–45.

Doorley, T. "Start Growing, Keep Going." *WorldLink*, Mar.-Apr. 1998, pp. 56–65.

Doorley, T., and Burger, R. "A Time to Grow"; "Corporate Growth"; "Growth: Reaching the Stars." *Chief Executive*, Dec. 1995 (special suppl.).

Edelman, K. (ed.). *The Dynamics of Continuous Growth*. Publication No. 1128-95-CH. New York: Conference Board, 1995.

Fox, J. "How Washington Really Could Help." *Fortune*, Nov. 25, 1996, pp. 92–98.

Garone, S. (ed.). *Growth: Top Priority for Future Success*. Publication No. 1166-96-CH. New York: Conference Board, 1996.

Hart, M. (ed.). *Value-Creating Growth: Goals, Strategies, Foundations*. Publication No. 1201-97-CH. New York: Conference Board, 1997.

Henkoff, R. "Growing Your Company: Five Ways to Do It Right." *Fortune*, Nov. 25, 1996, pp. 78–88.

Knobel, L., Clark, A., and Harris, F. "Growth Table Manners." *WorldLink*, Mar.-Apr. 1996, 47–53.

Lucenko, K. (ed). *How Growth Creates Value: Aligning Your Enterprise*. Publication No. 1224-98-CH. New York: Conference Board, 1998.

Lucier, C., and Asin, A. "Toward a New Theory of Growth." *Strategy & Business*, Winter 1996, pp. 10–16.

Mehta, K., Miller, H., and Read, M. "Seven Stars to Follow." *WorldLink*, Mar.-Apr. 1998, pp. 61–65.

Moeller, B., Tucker, J., and Devereaux, R. The Next Wave: Reengineering for Growth. *Strategy & Business*, Winter 1996, pp. 18–29.

Norton, R. "Exploding the Myths About Growth." *Fortune*, Nov. 25, 1996, pp. 76–77.

Sager, I. "How IBM Became a Growth Company Again." *Business Week*, Dec. 9, 1996, pp. 154–162.

Shao, M. "Beyond Reengineering: Now That Corporate America Has Been Downsized, Consultants Are Looking for a New Doctrine to Pitch." *Boston Globe*, Nov. 12, 1995, p. A121.

White, J. "Next Big Thing: Reengineering Gurus Take Steps to Remodel Their Stalling Vehicles." *Wall Street Journal*, Nov. 26, 1996, p. A1.

Wysocki, B. "The Outlook: 'Restructuring' Is Out, Replaced by 'Growth.'" *Wall Street Journal*, Dec. 9, 1996, p. A1.

"Global Corporate Strategies: Creating the Culture for Growth." *EIU (Economist Intelligence Unit) Crossborder Monitor*, Sept. 25, 1996, p. 1.

Appendix C

Takeaways

Notes

Introduction

1. These data are drawn from a set of ongoing analyses performed by our Growth Team. The shareholder value analysis is based on analyses of public companies in North America, Europe, and the Asia-Pacific region. To ensure comparability, Standard & Poor's Compustat has been our basic data source for financial information. The product/service innovation data were drawn from our surveys, for example, the *Survey of American Business Leaders*, sponsored by Deloitte & Touch LLP and Wirthlin Worldwide (May 1996), and confirmed by client data. Employee satisfaction data came from internal surveys done by clients and in our own firm. The job creation data are based on the rate of job growth within our group of the two hundred fastest-growing public companies. Using Compustat data on public companies, we found that the two hundred fastest growing companies (less than 2 percent of the total) created 32 percent of all jobs created by public companies. Against total job creation, including government, education, and so forth, these companies accounted for 12 percent of all job growth.

2. This list of companies is representative of the full list, which at this writing is closer to seventy-five companies. The data cover corporate/companywide information, as well as information from sector, divisional, and other business units.

3. Our analysis of growth patterns incorporated 1,920 companies. We followed their growth from 1976 through 1996.

4. T. Smart, "Jack's Encore," *Business Week*, Oct. 28, 1996, pp. 154–160.

5. The concept of the "growth wall" is, of course, not precise. We use two designators, number of employees and dollar revenues, although we believe the first to be more relevant, as the number of employees corresponds with the level of complexity. Complexity and the ability to deal with it define the growth wall.

6. J. Kass, R. Friedman, J. Leserman, P. Zuttermeister, and H. Benson, "Health Outcomes and a New Index of Spiritual Experience," *Journal for the Scientific Study of Religion*, 1991, 30, 203–211.

Chapter One

1. A. Manchon, Braxton Associates' *Survey of Canadian Corporate CEOs* (Oct. 1996); Deloitte & Touch LLP and Wirthlin Worldwide, *Survey of American Business Leaders* (May 1996).

2. *Economist* Intelligence Unit, *New Millennium Survey*. Interim data were available to us during the summer of 1998. The complete survey was scheduled to be released at year-end.

3. American Management Association, *Change Management: A Survey of Major U.S. Corporations* (New York: American Management Association, 1995).

4. T. Doorley, "Start Growing, Keep Going," *WorldLink*, Mar.-Apr. 1998, pp. 56–65.

5. Data are based on 3,978 companies sourced from Compustat. Growth Team analyst Matthew Marolda provided market-value growth calculations. The observation that returns are higher, independent of growth, as companies become larger is rooted in the market's view of scale. Small companies are seen as more volatile, so are assigned higher cost of capital. Thus, they require higher levels of profitability (returns above their cost of capital). Larger companies are seen as more stable; thus, the inverse applies.

6. Total return to shareholders is defined as the rate of growth of market value (share price adjusted for stock splits and so forth) plus dividends paid. This chart was first calculated by Growth Team consultant Daniel Ames and subsequently updated by Growth Team analyst Geoffrey Willison.

7. Analysis term and methodology are the same as in note 5.

8. Both examples represent actual client companies. From time to time we have camouflaged the identity of specific companies in order to use otherwise confidential data.

9. See note 8.

10. J. Donovan, R. Tully, and B. Wortman, *The Value Enterprise: Strategies for Building a Value-Based Organization* (Toronto: McGraw-Hill Ryerson, 1998).

11. This section is adapted from a presentation by Tom Doorley and dialogue with the World Economic Forum's Global Growth Company meeting, Oct. 11, 1998, in Singapore. At the time, most Asia-Pacific countries were mired in a deep economic slowdown and Western economies seemed to be on the brink.

Chapter Two

1. Our methodology for this analysis focused on contrasts between the extremes, that is, the high-growth/high-return companies versus their opposites, the low-growth/low-return group. This contrast provided the most vivid description of the differences in characteristics and behaviors. We created our contrasting groups from our value-growth matrix, Figure 1.1.

2. American Management Association, *Change Management*.

3. For this comparison we used year-end 1997 revenues for both companies. Microsoft's market value was as of year-end 1997. Apple's peak market value was year-end 1991. Apple's market value was adjusted for inflation to allow a truer comparison.

Chapter Three

1. Bob Edmonston, presentation at the Third Annual Growth Conference, presented by The Conference Board and sponsored by Deloitte Consulting/Braxton Associates, June 4–5, 1997. Edmonston's comments are summarized in M. Hart (ed.), *Value-Creating Growth: Goals, Strategies, Foundations*. Publication No. 1201-97-CH (New York: Conference Board, 1997).

Chapter Four

1. Quotes and notes from interview with Jim Koch, Mar. 1997.

2. The companies depicted here are intended to be representative of companies at various stages of the growth cycle. As a strategic-level illustration, our clients tell us the graphic works. However, within any specific company, individual products and services will likely fall into all phases of the cycle. At any one time all companies are in flux.

3. Quotes and notes from interviews with Gary Forsee, president of Sprint Long Distance, Oct.-Nov. 1996.

4. With liberal poetic license and paraphrase of actual conversations, the authors thank Sue Ellen and Scott for their enthusiastic role playing.

5. J. D. Power and Associates, 1998 *Residential Long-Distance Customer Satisfaction Study* (Los Angeles: J. D. Power and Associates, 1998).

6. J. Keller, "Streamlined: The Old Phone System Is Facing an Overload, So Sprint Has a Plan," *Wall Street Journal*, June 2, 1998, p. A1.

7. *Men's Health* celebrated its tenth anniversary with a double issue in August 1998.

8. T. Collins and T. Doorley, *Teaming Up for the '90s* (Burr Ridge, IL: Business One Irwin, 1991). The book is available in English, French, and Japanese.

9. Braxton Associates Alliance Survey, 1991.

10. From "Introducing the *Analyst 25*," *Alliance Analyst*, July 24, 1995, pp. 14–15, and "The Solo Flyers," *Alliance Analyst*, Aug. 7, 1995, pp. 18–19.

Chapter Five

1. Our Growth Team analysis identified these nineteen descriptors (out of one hundred specific characteristics) as having the highest correlation to the attributes of our value-creating growth benchmarks.

2. This chart is an industry-level view of the primary operational and infrastructure processes for a high-tech manufacturer. It had been

developed, at much greater levels of detail, by the Deloitte Consulting Reengineering for Results development team.

3. American Management Association, *Change Management.*

4. The general description of architecture and the specific example of Boeing are drawn from more than a decade of work with Professor Quinn. A specific source for more detail is his book, *The Intelligent Enterprise* (New York: Free Press, 1992).

5. Background on Ford 2000 provided by John Sieg, Ford's growth manager, in May and Aug. 1997.

6. Presented by Bob Teufel at the Second Annual Growth Conference, presented by The Conference Board and sponsored by Deloitte Consulting/Braxton Associates, Apr. 29–30, 1996.

7. M. Fradette and S. Michaud, *The Power of Corporate Kinetics: Create the Self-Adapting, Self-Renewing, Instant-Action Enterprise* (New York: Simon & Schuster, 1998).

8. To obtain the data, send your request in writing on your letterhead to Ms. Janice Z. Schneider, Deloitte Consulting/Braxton Associates, 200 Clarendon Street, 20th floor, Boston, MA 02116. Requests submitted in other ways cannot be honored.

9. The basic methodology for the benchmarks was the Growth Foundation Survey designed and maintained by the Growth Team. The survey triggers broad data collection and provides the structure for personal interviews.

10. The actual company camouflaged here hit its own growth wall early in 1997, well before the "Asian flu" took hold in early 1998 and while its competitors were continuing to enjoy high growth rates.

Chapter Seven

1. Notes and remarks by Walter M. Miller, senior vice president for strategy and development, at Becton-Dickinson and Company, Feb. and June 1998.

2. Survey results were presented to the participants at the Growth Conference. A copy of the presentation is available by contacting Janice Schneider in writing at Deloitte Consulting/Braxton

Associates, 200 Clarendon Street, 20th floor, Boston, MA 02116. Requests submitted in other ways cannot be honored.

Chapter Eight

1. George Bodway's remarks at the conference are summarized in Hart, *Value-Creating Growth*.

Chapter Nine

1. R. Buzzell, B. Gale, and R. Sultan, "Market Share: A Key to Profitability," *Harvard Business Review*, Jan.-Feb. 1975, p. 97.

2. Robert Browning, "Cleon," line 114.

Index